FAST ▶▶ FORWARD

LEVEL 4 TO LEVEL 5

SUE HACKMAN

Hodder & Stoughton
A MEMBER OF THE HODDER HEADLINE GROUP

Contents

The contents chart below reflects the different ways that this book can be used. Firstly, by looking *down each column*, you can see what each unit consists of and work your way through the book accordingly. Secondly, by looking *across each row*, you are able to follow each strand for particular emphasis in that area, concentrating on one of the strands and using the relevant parts of each unit. For example, to work on 'Writing Skills' follow the row across and simply use the page references to go to the specific sections of each unit.

Assessment Packs and other *Fast Forward* Books

Please note that Assessment Packs are available providing short 'before and after' tests for pupils aiming to move from one level to the next. These tests provide teachers with useful pupil profiles and provide pupils with clear targets. Assessment Packs are available for each of the *Fast Forward* books listed below.

Fast Forward Level 3 to Level 4	**ISBN 0340 74932 6**
Fast Forward Level 3 to Level 4 Assessment Pack	**ISBN 0340 78025 8**
Fast Forward Level 4 to Level 5	**ISBN 0340 78902 6**
Fast Forward Level 4 to Level 5 Literacy Assessment Pack	**ISBN 0340 80363 0**
Fast Forward Level 5 to Level 6	**ISBN 0340 78904 2**
Fast Forward Level 5 to Level 5 Literacy Assessment Pack	**ISBN 0340 80366 5**

This book offers an intensive programme for raising pupils from Level 4 to Level 5 in literacy. It is a resource for teachers who have been charged with accelerating pupils' progress over a short period, lifting them from competent personal reading and writing to a stage of confidence and control in managing language in more public contexts.

It takes a minimum of 30 hours to deliver, though there are opportunities to build extra work into the units, or to select out particular strands.

Secure standards require consolidation, application in different contexts and a continual process of ratcheting up pupils' skills. No book can do all this. What you have here is a core of basic lessons to bring into focus the skills that move a Level 4 to a Level 5.

If you are using this book to sharpen pupils for a test, then you may find it useful to cast ahead to the *Art of Analysis* strands of *Fast Forward: Level 5 to Level 6* which are designed to teach test style.

What is involved in getting to Level 5?

In the move from Level 4 to Level 5, the pupil must consolidate existing skills and add new ones:

In reading:

- Scour and select significant points
- Have a sharp sense of what is implied and how
- Justify and illustrate their opinions
- Synthesise diverse information.

In writing:

- Expression is more mature and interesting
- Expression is formal when it needs to be
- The complex sentence is well under control and confidently punctuated
- Writing is shapely, well-organised and signposted
- Irregular spellings are coming under control.

At Level 4, the pupil is already a fluent reader who can pick up more obvious hints from the writer to read beyond the literal, and in writing, he or she is able to extend a basic sentence, choosing words for effect and spelling accurately most regular spellings. In other words, the pupil at Level 4 is just beginning to understand their power over language and beginning to wield it.

But at Level 5, this budding reader and writer moves from personal experimentation and turns a face to the wider audience. Their work becomes more formal, their attitude to language becomes more manipulative and their new skills are put to work quickly into everyday tasks. Language is brought under the leash.

In reading, he or she has a strong sense of gist and a feel for the tone of the text, but is now able to pinpoint exactly how it has been created. There is a much stronger sense of the text as something that has been fashioned and composed. Level 5 readers can see beyond the text to the making of it – a fact that is enormously useful in informing their own writing.

Furthermore, they are much more assertive over the material they read. Rather than just collecting up relevant information, they are intelligently recasting it and shaping it for their own needs. Synthesising information, even where the sources are dissimilar and not easily combined, is one of the hallmarks of Level 5. Level 5 readers make use of reading in a more conscious and manipulative way: they are bringing order to their own knowledge and their own knowing.

In writing, something similar is in progress. Control is the key feature of Level 5 writing. Pupils move beyond the stage of simply 'expressing themselves' well to being more manipulative and truly creative: they make conscious choices with an eye on the reader, and have a new passion for order. There is something of the control freak in a level 5 writer.

The thing that will strike the teacher reading Level 5 work is a new maturity of expression, a literariness in the language. It is the magical effect of the complex sentence. The pupil who takes command of the complex sentence has entered a new phase of language that will propel them all the way to adulthood in writing. The sentence is it. The sentence is the single most important thing to teach about writing for pupils at this level. Text structures are largely laid down by convention; spellings are laid down before you are born; but the sentence is all yours – a playground of meaning, infinitely malleable, pregnant with infinite possibilities. When you can manage the complex sentence, you can mean what you want, you can mean new things. If you are sitting today knowing that you have pupils in your class who can turn a good sentence but lack joy and enthusiasm for language, then the complex sentence has the power to unlock the voice.

The task of the teacher is to skill up this growing reader and writer. In many ways, Level 5 is one of the easiest levels to teach because you are inducting pupils into some specific 'teachable' skills, and even better, these skills can be put to use immediately in every school day. Summary, note-taking, synthesising information, justification, expressing thoughts with sophistication (to take just a few) – these are the very skills that are needed across the curriculum.

About the structure of this book

This book is divided into ten units which take a minimum of three hours each to deliver. Each unit is divided into six sections, each one presented as a double page spread and taking around half an hour of curriculum time.

 1 Word Work

This section contains three parts:

- Spellings to learn: a list of subject spellings featuring high-frequency words that are complex and often misspelt. Pupils learn this list and are tested on it in the following unit.

- Know the difference: highlights common confusions in word use or spelling.

- Words at work: builds vocabulary for writing particular types of text, and pays particular attention to widening the range of connectives.

This section on word level work is placed first and broken into sections to encourage a focused, quickfire, challenging, high-pressure teaching approach to kick off the unit. It may well be taught as an oral whole-class activity, drawing the pooled knowledge of the class to derive rules, examples and suggestions. This should be the opposite of the quiet start.

2 Detective Reader

This section aims to formalise judgements about texts and show pupils how to find and present evidence. In effect, it is teaching basic literary criticism and how to present ideas in a test situation. It draws on the active reading strategies of the competent reader, and models at least once how to search for an answer and then formulate a response. Later sections also tackle the problem of what to do when one is stuck for an answer. It can be taught quite easily as a traditional lesson, or pursued in groups.

 3 Writing Skills

This section deals with writing skills at paragraph level. It covers summary, including note-taking, and the organisation of effective paragraphs. Both these skills are critical for examination, not because they are tested directly but because relevant answers are always concise and well-focused. Summary is more than mere shortening: it is also selecting and finding the true heart of the matter. The ideal way to teach these sections is by doing an example together as a whole class, so that the process of selection and wording is visible to pupils, then asking them to try the next example in twos and threes so that first attempts can be shared and compared. The emphasis is on showing how to do it.

 4 The Art of the Writer

This section moves pupils on from story planning to more sophisticated narrative techniques. Its focus is on storytelling and the management of the reader's responses. Thus, it addresses both reading and writing, and is a sister section to

Detective Reader. It can be delivered as a traditional lesson or in groups.

 5 Writing Style

This section takes a new approach to helping pupils to improve their writing at sentence level. It is arranged in two parts. The first part takes an interesting sentence and explores its structure, along with one or two other sentences organised in the same way. The structure is analysed and then borrowed by the pupils, who try it on for size. The idea is to give pupils experience of what it feels like to write a complex sentence, to add this particular sentence to a repertoire of sentence structures they can use, and to explain how the punctuation works. It is a real alternative to punctuating given sentences or expecting them to simply 'catch' complexity of expression from great writers. There is too much evidence that they do not.

The first part is best taught as a whole class activity, with the sentences displayed on the board for teacher-led analysis, and then quiet moments for writing which is then pooled for discussion.

The second part is best pursued in groups because it usually works by investigation or research of one aspect of the work already completed in the first part, e.g. the use of semi-colons.

 6 Non-fiction

This section takes a fresh look at some of the more challenging aspects of dealing with non-fiction texts. It is partly about how to make efficient use of them, and also about developing them in writing. Particular attention has been paid to

managing information that is diverse, e.g. it is embedded within different text types and has to be extracted and reframed with other information. This section can be used with the whole class, as long as opportunities are provided for individuals and groups to try the later exercises themselves before examples are pooled.

Last word

No book can do it all. Real teachers can take the ideas and make them work for their pupils. Real teachers can watch and tweak, unpack and explain, develop a point and try again, offer advice and feedback, adapt, extend, develop, articulate and think on their feet. No book can do all this. Use the book to suit you and your class. Books offer ideas and starting points: what teachers do best is teach.

Sue Hackman

November 2000

FAST ▶▶
FORWARD

▶▶▶▶▶

WORD WORK

Spellings: English

Learn these tricky spellings for use in English lessons:

1 Author
2 Audience
3 Rhythm
4 Rhyme
5 Character
6 Scene
7 Playwright
8 Theatre
9 Onomatopoeia
10 Poetry
11 Dialogue
12 Speech

Rhythm Helps You To Hear Music

Puzzle:

Find hidden in the list above something you would:

• do with a telephone

• wipe your feet on

• use as a diary

• do on a stage

• do in a restaurant.

Congratulations to the group that finds the most number of other hidden words.

Check your answers on page 130.

Know the difference: Practice or practise?

Practice is a noun

A dental practice

The tennis practice

The practice of medicine

Practise is a verb

To practise swimming

We practise medicine

I practise my football skills

To PractiSe Swimming – A way to remember that S signifies the verb.

Can you think of any other nouns that change 'C' to 'S' when they become verbs?
Check your answers on page 130.

Words at work:
Words to use when you want to disagree

On the contrary, …	Some people would find that …
On the other hand, …	In contrast, …
Conversely, …	I disagree.
However, …	There is another way of looking at this.
Some people would say …	The evidence points another way.

Can you think of others?

Work out the golden rules of disagreeing with someone. Here is a list of NEVERs.

1 Never be rude.

2 Never dismiss arguments as stupid.

3 Never assume your own opinion is obviously right.

4 Never rely on hearsay.

DETECTIVE READER

Working out the main point

Explanation:

Searching for the main point is a bit like using a metal detector on a beach. It can be easy to find, or buried so you have to dig a bit deeper.

How to spot the main point:

- The main point is often – but not always – given in the first and last lines of a paragraph.

- The main point is the hook on which all the other information hangs, so everything else extends or develops this point.

- The main point is often given emphasis in some way.

- The main point is often a general statement rather than an example, quote or detail.

Building on to the main point

The main point can be explained or developed in a number of ways. For example:

- through examples or illustration

- by explaining it in more detail

- by saying what happens next

- by discussing issues raised by the main point.

Find the main point in this extract, and then explain how the other information relates to it:

> It isn't unusual for film-goers to imagine that they are the film stars they have just been watching when they leave the cinema. Superstars like Tom Cruise, Bruce Willis and Pierce Brosnan leave a big impression on film fans. Half the men interviewed in a recent survey admitted that after watching an action film they are more likely to drive faster on the way home to try to recreate the thrills they have just watched on the silver screen.

Check your answer on page 130.

Building up to the main point

Here is another passage in which two important points are made: the first is where you might expect it to be, at the beginning of the paragraph. Where is the other?

> In July more rain fell on the village than ever before. As the skies thickened and rumbled, a record two inches fell each night for a week. Terrified villagers, who had never seen anything like it before, were forced to abandon their homes to the merciless waters of the swollen rivers which rolled effortlessly into their downstairs rooms. Catherine knew it was her fault.

Check your answer on page 130.

- How does the writer draw our attention to the second point?

- Look at the rest of the information in the paragraph. The links between it and the first point are made obvious. But the writer has left it to the reader to make the link to the second point.

The main point depends on why you need it

The writer's main point may not be the same as the reader's. It all depends on what the reader is reading for.

Here is the diary entry of a boy living in a castle in medieval England:

> **March 3rd, 1285, Saturday**
> Have been neglectful of my journal of late, for studies and other tasks fill the daylight hours when it is light enough to write. I made this entry in school while I did pretend to be studying my numbers.
>
>   At the butts yesterday one of the archers showed me why his kind are so feared by our King's foes. With bow in hand he stood before a tree with a trunk thicker than my chest. He pulled back the bow string until the veins stood out upon his face, and when he loosed the arrow its head passed clean through the tree trunk and pierced the other side. Seeing this, the other archers jeered that he was showing off, and four more of them repeated his trick. But when he let fly thirteen arrows in a minute none took up his challenge to better him.

From *Castle Diary* by Richard Platt and Chris Riddell

Activity

Write, in your own words, what the main point of the entry would be if you were:
- a military historian looking for information about medieval war
- writing a history of childhood.

WRITING SKILLS

Note-taking

If you take notes to remind yourself of the main things you have learnt, then your notes must be:

- quick to make
- clearly organised
- quick and easy to read even after a long time
- the important stuff.

To clear the clutter of words you can:

- just note the main points
- abbreviate to keep notes short and to the point.

In this way you can cut down the number of words without losing the meaning.

Abbreviations

Abbreviations are shortened forms of words or phrases. They are very useful for note-taking. You already know many abbreviations:

e.g.	=	for example
%	=	percent
Dr.	=	doctor

What do these mean?

| & | @ | a.m. | < | > | etc. | anon. | PC |

You can also make your own abbreviations by shortening common words, e.g.

fwd	=	*forward*
bwd	=	*backward*

Activity

- Suggest abbreviations for your school subjects, e.g. Gg, Hi.
- Suppose you are making notes about different countries for geography. What common words would you use, e.g. rainfall, economy? Make abbreviations for them.
- Suggest abbreviations for the names of different religions you have studied.

Shortening

You can also shorten full sentences to contain just enough words to still make sense.

This July was the wettest month of the year.

↓

July – wettest month this year.

This saves four words.

In the next sentence you could again cut out several words.

The rainfall in Manchester in the month of July was a surprising 22cms. In Edinburgh it was 10cms and in London just 7cms.

↓

Rainfall in Manchester in July surprising 22cms, Edinburgh 10cms & London 7cms.

Even better, you can lay it out to be even shorter and even clearer:

July rainfall

Manchester 22cms !!

Edinburgh 10cms

London 7cms

Or even more memorable:

Make notes on these passages:

The planet Mercury
Mercury is the small, rocky planet closest to the sun. It travels around the sun in 88 days, and spins round slowly on its axis in 59 days. Temperatures reach 400°F (204°C) on the side facing the sun, but the side facing away is bitterly cold at –170°F (–77°C).

The first underground service
The first underground train line opened in London in 1863 and was called the Metropolitan Line. It still exists today, but the trains have changed. The original trains were steam-powered and the tunnels were close to the surface. Now, the trains are electric and other lines are deep below the ground. America opened its first subway in 1897 in Boston.

THE ART OF THE WRITER

Openings

A writer has several jobs to do at the start of a novel or story:

- Introduce the characters.

- Set the scene in time and place.

- Start the plot rolling.

- Establish mood and tone.

- Establish the relationship between narrator and reader.

And above all…

- Hook the reader.

How a writer chooses to start a story will vary greatly – but all writers want to do the same thing: to make you read on. Read these openings and consider how they draw you in.

> Lizzy neither heard nor saw the bomb which hit her house. One moment it was just an ordinary Saturday afternoon and the next…

From *Lizzy's War* by Elisabeth Beresford

> When Bill Simpson woke up on Monday morning, he found he was a girl.
> He was standing staring at himself in the mirror, quite baffled, when his mother swept in.
> 'Why don't you wear this pretty pink dress?' she said.

From *Bill's New Frock* by Anne Fine

> Well, here I am again, sitting outside the Principal's office. And I've only been at the school for two days. Two lots of trouble in two days!

From *Pink Bow Tie* by Paul Jennings

It was sick and hungry and a long, long way from home. It had little brain but it sensed that the tank was a hostile environment and it cruised around the wall, revolving slowly about its axis, bumping the frost-rimed metal till it found the door.

From *Hydra* by Robert Swindells

Long, long ago, before time was caught and kept in clocks, there lived a king and queen. They ruled their kingdom wisely and well, but they did not often smile.

From *The Thistle Princess* by Vivian French

Activity

1 What do you learn in the opening lines about plot, time, place and character? Some of this information is given, and some you work out for yourself. Find examples of where you work out something for yourself.

2 Which openings make you want to read on? What makes you curious? Put the openings in order of interest.

3 Find some other fiction books and investigate the different ways of beginning a tale. Identify the tactics each book uses to hook the reader. For example:

- Writer uses surprise to engage the reader. (*Bill's New Frock*)

- The beginning is humorous. (*Bill's New Frock*)

- Opening establishes the setting. (*Pink Bow Tie*)

- The narrator is intriguing. (*Pink Bow Tie*)

4 Think of a fairy story you know very well, e.g. 'Little Red Riding Hood' and write four alternative openings for it such as the ones listed above. Share and compare your openings.

Don't tell your readers too much in your opening; drop hints for them to think about as they read the rest of the story.

WRITING STYLE

A sentence to borrow: pulling a punch

> When she smiles like that she shows all her teeth. They aren't her real teeth.

From *Are You There, God? It's Me, Margaret* by Judy Blume

Explanation:

- The main clause or basic sentence is: *she shows all her teeth*.

- The subordinate clause is: *when she smiles like that*. It only makes sense when it is put with the main clause. It is therefore a subordinate clause. Putting a subordinate clause at the beginning of the sentence makes a refreshing change.

- The follow-up sentence is: *They aren't her real teeth*. It starts with a pronoun to remind us that it still concerned with the people or things in the first sentence. It is deliberately short, like the punchline of a joke.

Similar sentences:

When Terry practises disco dancing he flails every limb. He is not a pretty sight.

When Uncle gets angry he turns bright red and splutters. He looks like an angry buffalo.

Activity

Try writing a formula to represent the two sentences at the bottom of the page 18. You could start:

| When | $+$ | subordinate clause ... |

Devise **three** more sentences that use this pattern.

Investigation: Pronouns

Find 100 words in the middle of a novel.

Pick out all the pronouns.

Activity

1 Work it out
   • What is the job of a pronoun?
   • How do you know who (or what) the pronoun refers to?

2 Experiment
   • Convert all the nouns to pronouns, then read the passage aloud.
   • Why can't you just keep on calling things by their pronouns?
   • What advice can you give about when to use the noun and when to use the pronoun?

The pronouns are:

I

You (This can mean one person or it can mean more than one)

He

She

It

We

They

NON-FICTION

Reading the page

Read the following text from a science book.

Thirsty flower

How much water does a plant need to stay fresh and alive? By giving a flower coloured water, you will see how good plants are at sucking up water through their stems.

You will need:

Fresh, white flower   Rubber band

Narrow vase of water   Cooking oil   Food colouring or ink

The oil floats on top of the water. It stops any water escaping into the air.

The water has travelled up the stem to the petals.

1 Add several drops of food colouring to the vase of water.

2 Gently pour the oil onto the water. Put the rubber band around the vase.

3 Put the flower in the vase. Move the rubber band so that it marks the top of the oil.

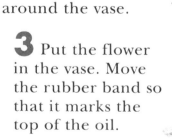

4 Leave the flower in a warm place for about two days.

The flower has sucked up this much water.

Desert plants
Cacti are able to live in dry deserts. They store the water that they take up from the soil.

On a blank sheet of paper, draw a diagram of the page opposite with boxes showing how the text is arranged in blocks. Draw blocks for: heading, introduction, instructions, list, explanation.

Afterwards, in a brightly coloured pen, draw a long arrow to show which way the eye should travel to make sense of this page.

Activity

1 Find the instructions section and answer these questions about its features:
   • Describe the way this section is laid out or arranged. How are you meant to read it?
   • Identify the verbs. What do you notice about the choice and position of the verbs in sentences?
   • What are the photographs for?
2 Find the first sentence of the introduction and the first sentence of the explanation. Find a word to describe each one and explain why the writer chose to open each section that way.
3 Who exactly is 'you' in the introduction, and how do you know?
4 What link does the reader have to make between the instructions and the sudden appearance of a desert plant? Add in a new sentence making this link clear.

In order to answer these questions you had to read on three levels:

Text level: how the information is organised.

Sentence level: how the information is expressed.

Word level: how the words are chosen, presented and spelt.

Good readers have strategies for getting the most out of a page like this. Where did you use:

● Scanning, or running your eyes over the page to see how it was arranged.

● Skimming or reading the text quickly to find out what it was about and how it was written.

● Searching for key words and phrases.

● Matching text and pictures.

● Re-reading to check you had got it.

● Making a link between this information and knowledge you already had.

● Remembering other pages like this, and how they worked.

WORD WORK

Spellings: History

First, test each other on the English spellings from Unit 1. Next, learn these tricky spellings for use in History lessons:

1 Government
2 Parliament
3 Conquer
4 Emperor
5 Reign
6 Foreign
7 Monarch
8 Democracy
9 Aristocracy
10 Policy
11 Chronological
12 Current
13 Independence
14 Military
15 Political
16 Siege

A way to remember the A.

Puzzle

- Can you find 20 ready-made words within these words, e.g. **over** in g**over**nment?

- Find three other words besides **reign** and **foreign** that contain **eign**.

Check your answers on page 130.

Know the difference: English and American spellings

English	American
colour	color
favourite	favorite
programme	program
centre	center
traveller	traveler

How do American spellings vary from English? For example, Americans often simplify 'OU' to 'O'. Check your answers on page 130.

Do you know any words which are different in America?

e.g.

English	American
pavement	sidewalk
nappy	diaper

Words at work: Giving instructions

Words to use when you want to give instructions:

First, …	Before _____ing,
Next, …	After _____ing,
Secondly, …	During the _____,
Thirdly, … (and so on)	Whilst you _____,
Finally, …	As you _____,

All these sentence starters help the reader to know *when* and *in what order* to do things.

Activity

Now try using some of these phrases to instruct someone how to:

1 Change a duvet cover.

2 Make a cup of tea.

3 Take school dinners for the first time.

DETECTIVE READER

Supporting evidence

Readers make judgements and form opinions about all sorts of things when they read. For example, they like or dislike characters, get an impression of what a place is like and feel strongly about issues and events. The easy job is stating your impression. For example:

A. *Jonah is a cold-hearted and selfish man.*

B. *Hardstone is a harsh environment.*

The harder job is to explain where you got this impression, finding evidence to justify your views. To do this, you can:

● Mention actions or events that prove your point.

● Quote words or phrases that create the impression.

For example:

A. *Jonah is cold-hearted and selfish man, as we see in his treatment of Leila and the theft of Mona's pocket money.*

B. *Hardstone is a harsh environment. Not only is the weather 'cold as knives' but the camp is completely surrounded by 'frozen tundra' and 'empty even of shrubs and couchgrass'. Even the staff are described as 'glacial'.*

Try it

Now you try it. What impression do you get of Uncle from this description of his garage?

> His uncle's garage was not at all as he'd expected. Bits of old engines were piled in one corner and shelves of boxes, all labelled, lined the back wall. Framed yellowing photographs of his uncle on different motorbikes were scattered around. On the bench, gleaming screwdrivers, spanners and other tools lay lined up like old proud soldiers on parade in height order. In the centre of the garage was the winning motorbike.

Compare your answer with that on page 130.

In the next extract, the subject is much trickier because there are mixed messages about the main character. It's best to say this directly and explain the conflicting views you have of him, providing evidence. If you feel confident, you can end by giving your more definite impression.

A powerful-looking man in his sixties, wearing a beautifully tailored linen suit and holding a panama hat, stood on the gallery above and looked down over the iron railing.

His grey hair was brushed neatly back from his smooth, tanned, barely wrinkled forehead. His eyes were large, dark and long-lashed and intense, and every minute or so his sharp, dark-pointed tongue peeped out at the corner of his lips and flicked across them moistly. The snowy handkerchief in his breast pocket was scented with some heavy cologne like those hot-house plants so rich you can smell the decay at their roots.

From *The Subtle Knife* by Philip Pullman

You could use these starters:

The man is puzzling. On the one hand he is …, yet on the other he is …

The reader is reassured by…

Yet there are hints that he is also …

The overall impression is that he is …

In the following passage, the narrator has just been attacked by the school bully. He is being looked after by his friend Minty and her Mum. What impression do you get of Minty's Mum and how is this impression formed?

I looked round the room. It was jam-packed with all brightly painted things, curiosities and funniosities, shabby and tatty books and flowers everywhere and old dolls and toys on chests and tables and pictures and clowns and battered trains and trays – everywhere covered, everything coloured, a grown-up's toy shop. Three ginger cats watched me eat.

"Here," said her mum. "These should fit. I can mend your blazer and the shirt but not the trousers."

"But you can't buy me …"

"Yes, I can. Don't argue. You'll only lose."

"But dad'll kick up …"

"Your dad's not taking much care of you. So I wouldn't worry about him too much …"

"He's all right really. It's just he only … thinks about his pictures."

"His pictures?"

"He paints. He's packed in his job so he can paint. We've moved a bit while he tries to …"

"Find himself …"

"Yes. How d'you know?"

"Oh, I know. I've been trying to do that for years but I keep getting away from me. Now why don't you two wander while I clear up a bit? Look, kid, you've got the palest face I've ever seen. Minty – I know, let's dig out some money and you and Owen go to the beach. On the train, Owen. It's wonderful. Much better than in the car. Not that we've got a car. How could I afford one? Have you been since you've been here?"

"No."

"Off you go, then. Wait, I'll have to get some money out of the marigold teapot, the electricity bill money, but we'll worry about that later. It's summer now, so who cares?"

From *Just Ferret* by Gene Kemp

WRITING SKILLS

When to start a new paragraph

The word **paragraph** comes from the early Greek word '**paragraphos**', which was a horizontal line used to divide written texts into units. However there was a time when texts had no divisions at all. Paragraphs as we know them were introduced by the early printers as a way of organising texts. Today, you can show a paragraph break by indenting the first line or by leaving a line between each paragraph. The main thing is that the break is clear to the reader.

Paragraphs are used to alert the reader when the writer has changed tack. A new paragraph indicates:

- a change in topic

- a change of viewpoint or person

- a jump in time

- a change of place

- a change of mood

- in dialogue, that someone else has started to speak.

Here is an extract of six paragraphs from the ancient story *Beowulf*. A monster is closing in on a group of warriors asleep in a hall.

What kind of change is indicated by each paragraph?

> Through the dark night a darker shape slid. A sinister figure shrithed down from the moors, over high shoulders, sopping tussocks, over sheep-runs, over gurgling streams. It shrithed towards the timbered hall, huge and hairy and slightly stooping. Its long arms swung loosely.
>
> One man was snoring, one mumbling, one coughing; all the Geats guarding Hereot had fallen asleep – all except one, one man watching.
>
> For a moment the shape waited outside the hall. It cocked an ear. It began to quiver. Its hair bristled. Then it grasped the great iron ring-handle and swung open the door, the mouth of Hereot. It lunged out of the darkness and into the circle of dim candlelight, it took a long stride across the patterned floor.
>
> Through half-closed eyes Beowulf was watching, and through bared teeth he breathed one word. 'Grendel.' The name of the monster, the loathsome syllables.
>
> Grendel saw the knot of sleeping warriors and his eyes shone with an unearthly light. He lurched towards the nearest man, a brave Geat called Leofric, scooped him up, with one ghastly claw, choked the scream in his throat. Then the monster ripped him apart, bit into his body, drank the blood from his veins, devoured huge pieces; within one minute he had swallowed the whole man, even his feet and hands.
>
> Still the Geats slept. The air in Hereot was thick with their sleep, thicker still with the death and the stench of the monster.'

Check your answers on page 131.

Here is an extract from an encyclopaedia. The original has six paragraphs. Can you work out where they start and why?

Musicals tell stories through words, songs, and dances. They can be either stage shows or films. Many are American, which is where the stage musical began, but others are written elsewhere: the well-known musicals *Evita* and *Cats* are both British. There are many different styles of musical. Some musicals are based on books or plays, for example *Oliver!*, which is based on the book *Oliver Twist*, and *West Side Story*, which is an updated version of Shakespeare's play *Romeo and Juliet*. Others have new stories especially written (called librettos), such as *Starlight Express* and the film *Grease*. Musicals began in the 19th century as operettas ('little operas'). In operettas, songs and spoken dialogue were used to tell stories that were often comic and fantastical, with elaborate stage sets and exotic costumes. The actual musical began in America in the late 1920s and 1930s in the heyday of dancers such as Fred Astaire. Dancing was more important in the musical than in operettas, and the stories were usually about ordinary people in modern clothes. The first film musical was made in 1927. Film-makers soon realized that they could do many things on film that were not possible on stage, and film musicals became all-singing, all-dancing extravaganzas. Fashions changed again in the 1940s. Stars such as Fred Astaire and Gene Kelly popularized a new kind of musical, in which the story was as interesting as the singing and dancing. In the 1970s costume and fantasy musicals once more became popular. In Andrew Lloyd Webber's *Starlight Express*, the performers play the part of trains, rushing around the stage on roller-skates.

From *The Children's Oxford Encyclopaedia*

Check your answers on page 131.

THE ART OF THE WRITER

Endings

At the end of a story, a writer usually wants to:

- Conclude the story.

- Tie up loose ends.

- Make the reader feel satisfied and settled.

- Draw out a moral or judgement on the characters.

There is no particular way that writers use to end their stories, but a weak ending can ruin a text for a reader. Here are some ways that stories can end:

- With a moral.

- By returning to the beginning (same setting, character, even the same words).

- With a happy event or celebration (e.g. lovers re-united).

- A rite of passage (e.g. a birth, marriage or death).

- A hint of a sequel.

- Finding true love.

- A twist in the tale.

- A solution to a problem or puzzle.

- Good winning over evil.

Think of stories which end in any of these ways. You can include film and television programmes.

Writing towards an ending

Good writers usually know how their story will end before they begin to write. This helps them to plan the whole text. They plan their stories to build up towards the ending by way of key events or milestones. It is nearly always the behaviour of the characters that drives the plot towards the ending – things they say or do that throw the plot onto a new course.

For example, here is a real ending:

> Grandad headed for the door carrying his suitcase.
>
> Nurse Gribble started to shriek. 'Don't go, don't go. Don't leave me alone with this dragon.'
>
> Grandad looked at her. 'Don't be silly,' he said. 'There's no such thing as a dragon.'

From *There's No Such Thing* by Paul Jennings

Here are the milestone events which build towards it:

1 Grandad tells the nurse that he has seen a few unusual things in the hospital, but he is unwell and disorientated, and the nurse just thinks he is a silly old man.

2 Feeling much better, Grandad sees a dragon in the ward, befriends it and feeds it food from his dinner.

3 On the day he is due to leave, Grandad warns the nurse that the dragon has grown much bigger, and this time she is very rude to him.

Plan three milestone events for the two endings below.

> I left the clock on the mantelpiece. There it is! Inlaid with little mirrors and misty pearls. It's like a piece of icing done by a goddess, dropped out of heaven.

From *That's None of Your Business* by Kevin Crossley-Holland

> The ghost stood open-mouthed looking round the deserted library. I suppose it was the middle of the night in the ghost library too. He walked over to a long bookshelf and found a gap. Carefully he slid the book, *How to Live Forever,* into the gap. There was an unearthly sigh, like a whole forest of trees rustling their leaves. Then the ghost library started to waver and my room seemed to thicken.
>
> Just before he disappeared, Mr. Beresford turned and waved at me. He looked blissfully happy.
>
> 'Rest in peace,' I whispered.
>
> I hope he does. It sounds a lot nicer than living forever.

From *How to Live Forever* by Mary Hoffman

Predicting endings

One of the pleasures of reading is anticipating what will happen, and measuring your best guess against what actually happens. Here is the blurb from the back of *Forbidden Game* by Malorie Blackman. Predict the ending and the kind of milestone events you would expect to find.

> Shaun's parents never let him do anything. So when they finally say he can go on the school trip, he knows he's in for a great time. But a dangerous game goes horribly wrong and soon he's fighting for his life.

Write the last paragraph of the book. Afterwards, you could look up the ending in the original.

WRITING STYLE

A sentence to borrow: colons

> To be or not to be: that is the question.

From *Hamlet* by William Shakespeare

Explanation:

The first part of this sentence is an equal balance between 'To be' and 'not to be', joined by the conjunction 'or'. Making an equal join is the job of a conjunction.

The verb is written in the infinitive. Infinitives always start 'TO'.
For example:

To be

To stay

To kill

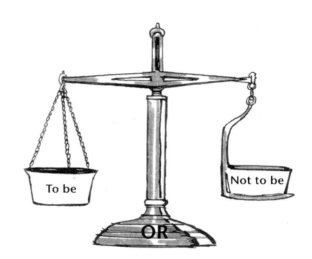

The colon is similar to the equal sign in mathematics (=). It means that the next part adds up to the same as the part before. It suggests that the second part mirrors the first, and is inseparable from it. You could quite easily put a full stop, but a colon leaves it in the same sentence and suggests that the two are so closely linked that you wouldn't want to separate them.

Devise a diagram that shows the weighting of the different parts of Hamlet's sentence above.

Similar sentences:

To stay and make William happy or to go and make herself happy: that was the choice facing Irma.

To kill or be killed: it was a straight choice.

Devise two more sentences which use the same structure.

Investigation: Colons and semi-colons

Activity

1 Search for colons and semi-colons in a novel.

2 Work out the job of colons and semi-colons. You will find more on semi-colons in Unit 7.

3 Experiment:
   Try borrowing the sentence structure of at least two sentences that use colons or semi-colons.

To do yourself

• Watch out for colons over the next few days.

• Try using some in your own sentences.

HELP

: = Colon

; = Semi-colon

NON-FICTION

Retrieving and collating information

A common task in everyday life is to research information and then to make a judgement. To do this you have to collect and compare similar information. The trick is to find a neat way of comparing or evaluating it.

Read the following text:

> The leaf-cutter bee, biting with her powerful jaws, will cut an oval shape from the edge of a rose leaf, roll it into a cylinder, and fly back to line her nest with it. She digs a tunnel in rotten wood to make her nest in – or finds a tunnel left by some other insect.
>
> Mining bees nest in the ground. There are more than 100 different species and they are especially useful in pollinating fruit trees. The female will burrow as much as 600mm into the ground. She digs with her front feet and her hind feet kick out the earth behind her.
>
> The cuckoo bee is a solitary bee but it looks like a bumble bee. It behaves like the cuckoo bird, in the way it lays its eggs. The female has no pollen. She carries sacs on her legs and so is unable to feed and care for her young. Instead she will try moving into a bumble bee's nest. The workers will attack her at first, but if she manages to stay, they begin to accept her as queen.
>
> There are sixteen species of bumble bee. They build up small colonies of up to a few hundred bees in the Spring after the queen has made a nest underground in an old mouse hole or similar hiding place.
>
> Honey bees live in permanent and very much larger colonies of up to 60,000 bees. They have been valued for their honey ever since early man took honey from wild nests. Nowadays they usually live in wooden hives and are looked after by a bee-keeper.
>
>

From *About Bees and Honey*, 1979

Activity

Take two minutes to discuss the organisation of the text.

- Give it an overall title, and a sub-heading for each paragraph.

- Describe how the paragraphs relate to one another – is it by order of event, importance, or something else?

Now take two minutes to agree answers to the following questions, and as you are doing this, notice how you go about it.

1 Write down three different places where bees build nests.

2 Which bee steals a bumble bee's nest?

3 Why does a cuckoo bee use other bees' nests?

What kind of reading did you do to answer each of these questions? In other words what skills did you use?

In order to answer these questions you had to:

- skim the text in order to find out what it was about and to understand the structure and the layout

- scan the text for key words and phrases

- re-read in order to check for details

- retrieve the relevant information.

To compare the bees, you have to find a way of arranging the details so that they can be compared easily. A table is a good way of compiling similar information because you can list the objects down one side, and the points of comparison along the top. Then you just drop the information into the right box.

Complete the table.

Type of bee	Location of nest	Method of nest building
The leaf cutter		Digs or finds a tunnel. Lines it with pieces of leaf
	Burrow under the ground	
		Steals bumble bee's nest
Bumble bee		
		Man made

Afterwards, discuss with others how you went about finding the information and filling in the boxes. Identify some useful shortcuts or tips.

WORD WORK

Spellings: Geography 1

First, test each other on the History spellings from Unit 2. Next, learn these tricky spellings for use in Geography lessons:

1. European
2. Asian
3. Mediterranean
4. Atlantic
5. Pacific
6. Arctic
7. Antarctic
8. Great Britain
9. Ireland
10. Country
11. Continent
12. Ocean

"No you fool, I said book a holiday to Ireland!!"

Know the difference

I see land!

A way to remember the difference.

Can you think of other countries with names that are homophones or homonyms?

- **Homophone** = word that sounds the same as another, but has a different spelling.

- **Homonym** = a word that is identical to another, but has a different meaning.

Check your answers on page 131.

An **island** is a place surrounded by water.

Ireland is the country.

34

Words at work: Giving directions

Here are some words to use when giving directions:

Go up/down/along/across

Proceed up/down/along/across

Continue up/down/along/across … until

Pass the _____ on your left/right.

At the _____ , turn …

Take the _____ turning on the left/right.

Turn left/right into _____ Road.

Bear left/right …

Keep to your left/right …

After _____ metres, …

Approximately …

Roughly …

You will see a …

Look for …

You will find the …

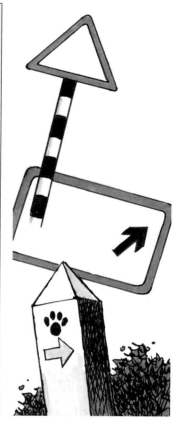

Activity

Now use some of these phrases to direct someone to:

1 Your home.

2 The Headteacher's Office.

3 The nearest sweet shop.

DETECTIVE READER

Quoting evidence

Sometimes you have to back up your views. To do this, you can mention events or better still you can quote the text. This means lifting words and phrases the writer has used. Picking the right quote is a useful skill.

Quotes should be:

- quite short

- where the writer uses a telling choice of words

- easier than putting it in your own words.

Example

Here is a passage about Sherlock Holmes. Notice the two quotations that have been picked out to support the views of the reader, below:

He is quickly assessing her for clues.

> With a resigned air and a somewhat weary smile, Holmes begged the beautiful intruder to take a seat and to inform us what was troubling her.
> "At least it cannot be your health," said he, as <u>his keen eyes darted over her</u>; "so <u>ardent a bicyclist</u> must be full of energy."
> She glanced down in surprise at her own feet, and I observed the slight roughening of the side of the sole caused by the friction of the edge of the pedal.
> "Yes I bicycle a good deal, Mr Holmes, and that has something to do with my visit to you today."

she has not told him – he has worked it out.

From *The Solitary Cyclist* by Sir Arthur Conan Doyle

We know Sherlock Holmes has great powers of observation because we are told 'his keen eyes darted over her'. He notices the scuffs on the soles of her shoes which tell him she is an 'ardent' bicyclist.

To write this up, one quotation has been used and the other one put mainly into other words. Why?

You try it

Find quotations in this extract to make the point that Perks is offended when the children hold a collection to buy him a birthday present:

> "So you've been round telling the neighbours we can't make both ends meet? Well, now you've disgraced us as deep as you can in the neighbourhood, you can just take the whole bag of tricks back where it came from. Very much obliged, I'm sure. I don't doubt you meant it kind, but I'd rather not be acquainted with you any longer if it's all the same to you." He deliberately turned the chair round so that his back was turned to the children. The legs of the chair grated on the brick floor, and that was the only sound that broke the silence.

From *The Railway Children* by E. Nesbit

Write up your point starting 'It is clear that Perks offended ….'

Also find quotations in the next extract that show how the narrator is upset to have lost the friendship of another castaway:

> He was not angry or sullen at me. But I knew I had hurt him to the soul. It wasn't that we didn't speak – we did – but we no longer talked to one another as we had before. We lived each of us in our separate cocoons, quite civil, always polite, but not together anymore. He had closed himself in his thoughts. The warmth had gone from his eyes, the laughter in the house was silenced. He never said so – he did not need to – but I knew that now he would prefer to paint alone, to fish alone, to be alone. So day after day, I wandered the island, hoping when I returned he might have forgiven me, that we could be friends again.

From *Kensuke's Kingdom* by Michael Morpurgo

Useful words when you use quotation:

- suggests
- implies
- paints a picture of
- creates a feeling of
- hints
- conveys

WRITING SKILLS

Paragraph cues

A cue is a signal. The paragraph break is itself a cue to the reader. It tells the reader that there has been a shift in topic, viewpoint or time. Good writers also provide other cues to alert the reader to the content of the paragraph. It helps the reader to get ready and look for the right things.

A writer can provide:

- a heading

- a key sentence which says what the rest will be about

- a verbal signal to the reader that signals a shift in time, viewpoint, etc.

Headings and key sentences

This short piece of writing has key sentences, but it has lost its paragraph breaks and headings.

Breathing helps us to absorb life-giving oxygen into our blood. It also helps to remove carbon dioxide from our blood. Our breathing speeds up when we exercise and slows down when we are resting. When we breathe we inhale, sucking air into our lungs. Oxygen in the air goes from the airspaces in our lungs and is absorbed into our blood. We blow air out of our lungs when we exhale. Waste carbon dioxide is taken from our blood into the air spaces in our lungs. We get rid of this waste by breathing out.

Activity

- Find the paragraph breaks and check that each one starts with a key sentence.

- Create one-word headings for each paragraph.

- Explain what a good key sentence does and why writers use it.

Check your answers on pages 131–2.

Signals about shifts

We have already seen that writers use paragraph spacing to indicate changes of time, place, topic, viewpoint or mood. But how do they signal the *type* of shift in words?

Here are the opening sentences from six paragraphs in a novel. There are 23 sentences in the whole extract. What can you work out about the content of the extract from these opening sentences?

1 By the time evening came the air was so still and heavy that Paul felt as if he needed to cut away chunks of it in order to move about in it.
2 He was on the sands when the first crack came.
3 He thought about the girl, and he began to run, the damp sand claggy already under the soles of his shoes.
4 By the time he reached the red rocks small rivers were gushing from them.
5 Rain pittered down from the overhang and washed over her skin.
6 He stood up, helpless, oblivious of the rain beating down on him.

In sentence 1,

- 'By the time evening came' warns us that time has moved on.

- The use of Paul's name warns us that we are now following his view of events.

Writers rarely mention names or time unless there is a shift, and readers assume that neither has changed unless they are told.

Activity

Go through each sentence and identify the signals to the reader about changes of time, viewpoint or anything else. Can you also find signs that tell the reader that something has *not* changed?

Activity

Write key sentences that signal shifts in these cases:

- You are explaining how to make bread sticks in the oven. Start the last of seven instructions, the one which makes a serving suggestion. How do you warn the reader that this is your last instruction and that it is not about cooking but about presenting the dish?

- You are writing a story about a robbery at a small bank. The three cashiers have been handcuffed and gagged. The gang have not seen the fourth cashier hidden under the desk, close to the police alarm button. You have been describing what the gang are up to, and now you want to let the reader in on the secret of the hidden person.

- You are describing your true-life journey across a desert. You are now up to the bit when there were days and days of the same thing, and you've already described it. How do you move on to the day you arrived at the oasis?

- Your main character has been pondering a dilemma, and this is the moment when he decides what to do. How do you communicate to the reader that the pondering is over and the decision is made?

THE ART OF THE WRITER

Narrators as characters

The narrator is important because the events are told from his or her perspective. The narrator can be a character in the story, too. Read this extract from the beginning of a novel and say what you can work out about the narrator:

They thought we had disappeared, and they were wrong. They thought we were dead, and they were wrong. We stumbled together out of the ancient darkness into the shining valley. The sun glared down on us. The whole world glistened with ice and snow. We held our arms against the light and stared in wonder at each other. We were scorched and blackened from the flames. There was dried blood on our lips, cuts and bruises on our skin. Our eyes began to burn with joy and we laughed, and touched each other and started to walk down together towards Stoneygate. Down there, our neighbours were digging for us in the snow. Policemen were dragging the river bed for us. The children saw us first and started running. Their voices echoed with astonishment and joy: Here they are! Oh, here they are! They clustered round us. They watched us as if we were ghosts, or creatures from some weird dream. Here they are! they whispered. Look at them. Look at the state of them!

Yes, here we were, the children who had disappeared, brought back into the world as if by magic: John Askew, the blackened boy with bone necklaces and paintings on him; Allie Keenan, the good-bad ice girl with silver skin and claws; the wild dog Jax; and me, Kit Watson, with ancient stories in my head and ancient pebbles in my palm.

From *Kit's Wilderness* by David Almond

Activity

1 Find three things that suggest that the narrator is injured.

2 Find two things that suggest that the narrator is overjoyed.

3 Find two things that suggest that the narrator has been somewhere dark.

4 Find three things that suggest that the narrator has had an unusual experience.

5 Think of other things that strike you about the narrator (e.g. age, feelings, sex, mental state), and point to details in the text that gave you this impression.

6 Read aloud the first nine sentences using the third person, e.g. *They thought they had disappeared, and they were wrong. They thought they were dead, and they were wrong.* Discuss how this changes the story.

Now read this opening and discuss your reactions to the narrator:

> Way back in Once Upon a Time time, I was making a birthday cake for my dear old granny.
>
> I had a terrible sneezing cold.
>
> I ran out of sugar.
>
> So I walked down the street to ask my neighbor for a cup of sugar. Now this neighbor was a pig.
>
> And he wasn't too bright either.
>
> He had built his whole house out of straw.
>
> Can you believe it? I mean who in his right mind would build a house of straw?
>
> So of course, the minute I knocked on the door...

What in this extract tells you that this is a new angle on a traditional character?

For a writer, there are advantages and disadvantages in using a first person narrator. What are they? Here is a list of advantages. Try filling in the disadvantages against each point.

First person narrator	
Advantages	Disadvantages
• The narrator can be a character in the story. • You see everything through their eyes. • You know what the character is thinking and feeling. • The story is told in their voice.	

Try writing one or two paragraphs told by an unusual narrator, e.g. Goldilocks from the point of view of Baby Bear.

WRITING STYLE

A sentence to borrow: starting with -ing

Looking over his shoulder, Skywalker could see the storm blast from the exploding planet rearing up behind him.

Similar sentences:

> **Curling around the ankles of his new owner, the cat reflected on the fickleness of humankind.**

> **Stooping to pick up the duvet, Mother noticed two large, pale, very dead feet protruding from beneath the bed.**

Explanation:

What makes these sentences unusual and interesting is that they each start with an 'ING' verb: Looking, Curling, Stooping.

- 'ING' verbs are known as non-finite verbs because the action is not a complete or finite action. The 'ING' makes it sound as though it is happening at the moment you read it.

- You also know that you will be told something more – what happened next. That bit comes after the comma.

- Notice the way the comma separates the opening from the main clause. You usually put a comma here.

- The main clause (this is the main part of the sentence, and here it comes after the comma) always starts with a noun or pronoun so you know right away who was involved.

This is an easy sentence to write. If you start with an 'ING' verb, the rest of the sentence looks after itself.

Activity

Complete these two sentences using the same pattern:

Looking . . . ., *(noun/pronoun)*. . . . .

Pausing to . . . ., *(noun/pronoun)* . . . .

Now try:

Without looking. . . . ., *(noun/pronoun)*. . . . .

Without pausing to . . . ., *(noun/pronoun)*. . . . .

Extending this idea

- What other words would go where *'without'* is placed? (e.g. Instead of…)

- Try starting similar sentences with verbs ending in 'ED', for example:

  Bored of waiting for the bus, Tania decided to walk home.

  Defeated, Harold's army fled.

There is a kind of shorthand in sentences starting with non-finite verbs. What we really mean is:

Because she was bored of waiting…

NON-FICTION

Synthesising information 1

Sometimes we have to draw together information from several places and weld it together in writing. The information doesn't always come in a form that you can easily join onto other information. It is a case of pulling together different types of information and rolling it together under new headings.

Your friend has written a worried letter explaining that his parents have almost decided to spend a year in Australia because there is a job there. Write a letter encouraging her to think of all the good things about Australia.

Here is the information you find about Australia:

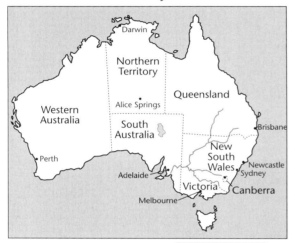

Australia has:
- dramatic landscapes
- unusual animals, some of them dangerous
- unspoilt beaches
- colourful cities
- dry, uninhabited deserts
- huge distances to travel between cities
- superb shops
- a wide range of restaurants
- friendly people
- a great climate

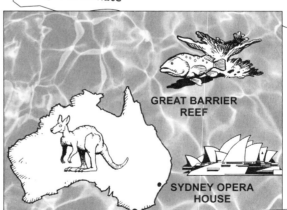

GREAT BARRIER REEF

SYDNEY OPERA HOUSE

Climate

- Summer – November to March is hot and humid with rain in the North (average daily temperature 31°C). Warm in the South (average daily temperature 27°C).
- Winter – June to August is warm in the North, West and East (average daily temperature 24°C). Cool and showery in the South (average daily temperature 15°C).

Currency & shopping

- currency: Australian dollar
- credit cards widely accepted
- tourist shops
- precincts
- open-air markets
- Aboriginal art

What to pack:
- ✓ dress for comfort
- ✓ lightweight clothes and shoes, sun hat
- ✓ sun glasses, sun cream
- ✓ jacket or sweater in winter
- ✓ formal outfit for special occasions
- ✓ passport and visitor's visa
- ✓ lightweight walking boots

Activity

None of the information will do just as it is, so the best way is to decide on your main points in advance, and then collect up information around them.

How to structure your letter in seven paragraphs:

1 Write an opening statement greeting your friend and explaining why you are writing.

2 Put the information into paragraphs organised around these ideas:

- the climate

- things to see

- things to remember

- a fourth paragraph on a topic chosen by you

- a fifth paragraph on a topic chosen by you.

3 Finish off with a suitable last paragraph that summarises some of your key points and wishes him well.

How to do it:

Now go through the information again, and as you come across something that fits into one of the headings, list it under that heading. Another way of doing this is to find five different ways of marking the text (e.g. underlining, circling, highlighting) and pick out information for each paragraph in this way. Other people like to number the information in the margin, e.g. a 2 in the margin means that this point belongs in paragraph 2.

Write and then swap your letter with someone else and mark them out of ten for these features (2 marks for each point):

1 Are there seven paragraphs organised as instructed?

2 Does each paragraph start with a key sentence that signals what it is about?

3 Is all the information encouraging for the friend?

4 Is the information in each paragraph linked and not just like a list?

5 Is the letter consistent in the way it talks to the reader like a friend?

WORD WORK

Spellings: Geography 2

First, test each other on the Geography 1 spellings from Unit 3. Then, learn these tricky spellings for use in Geography lessons:

1 Latitude
2 Longitude
3 Physical
4 Temperature
5 Climate
6 Neighbour
7 Agriculture
8 Industrial
9 Economy
10 Political
11 Social
12 Village

Experiencing the link between temper and temperature

Puzzle

How many words of five letters or more can you find within the words on this list?

Check your answers on page 132.

Know the difference: Tricky homophones

Series – different stories featuring the same characters, e.g. X Files.

Serial – a story in instalments, e.g. Eastenders.

Cereal – a crop such as wheat, oats, barley.

A way to remember:

• A <u>c</u>ereal is a <u>c</u>rop

• A <u>s</u>eries has <u>s</u>hort stories

• A seria<u>l</u> has <u>l</u>ong stories

What is the difference between:

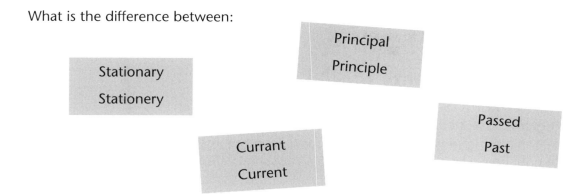

Stationary

Stationery

Principal

Principle

Currant

Current

Passed

Past

Check your answers on page 132 and then invent a way of remembering which is which.

Words at work: Explanations

Here are useful words to use when giving an explanation:

The reason for …	The effect of this is …
Another factor is …	Consequently …
A further factor is …	So, …
Because …	And so, …
Therefore …	A further consequence …
This causes …	Despite …
This in turn causes …	Inevitably …
As a result …	This has the effect of …
As a consequence, …	The end result is …

What other words are common to explanations? Look in a textbook for examples.

Activity

Now use some of these phrases by explaining what you know about:

1 The rain cycle.

2 The life cycle of an animal such as the salmon or butterfly.

Or

3 How global warming occurs.

DETECTIVE READER

Using words to create special effects

Authors choose words the way people choose clothes by trying on different garments until they find exactly the one that looks best and will make the right impression. Authors try out different words in a sentence until they find just the right one to create an effect on the reader.

For example, there is something special about the word *prowling* in this sentence:

> **The teacher came *prowling* along the rows of desks.**

The author has chosen this word because it has unusual associations:

When you write about special effects, you should:

- point out the word or phrase that creates the effect

- pinpoint what it makes the reader think of

- explain its impact and how well it works.

For example:

The author has used the word <u>prowling</u> to describe the teacher's movements. The word suggests that the teacher is a dangerous wild animal hunting for prey in the jungle. It implies that the teacher is searching for someone to tell off, creating a sense of tension.

Try it

- Search for four examples of 'special effect' words in the extract opposite, and write them in four circles.

- Draw branches from each circle and write against them all the associations you have with each word.

- Pick out one in particular to write about, explaining the effect of the word in context.

The floppy, untidy shape of a heron was scrambling straight up out of the reed beds. It did not flap away in stately slow motion, like an ordinary heron. It flailed and hoisted itself up, exactly as if it were bounding up an invisible spiral stair. Then, from a great height, it tumbled away towards the sea beyond the marsh. Something had scared it badly. But what? Something in the marsh had frightened it. And seeing the heron so frightened frightened Lucy.

From *The Iron Woman* by Ted Hughes

In the next extract, two children enter the cottage of a hermit called Birdman. Identify the 'special effect' words and complete a table like the one below.

By now the force of the storm was spent and the wind had died, but the sea was still seething and angry. The waves rolled into the bay from Samson, gathering and rearing as they neared the shore before they curled over to hurl themselves onto the hissing sand. The beach was empty.

A sudden gust of wind shook the cottage, rattled the windows and whistled down the chimneys disturbing the ash in the fire grate. I moved closer to Daniel who had picked up the end of the loaf on the bottom shelf to smell it.

"Wonder why he keeps four loaves?" he said. Then, as if they were all answering together, the birds lining the shelves began to shriek and scream at us. That was more than I could take. Dragging Daniel behind me I ran for the door which opened in front of us just as we reached it. Prince was suddenly around our legs, jumping up at us and shaking himself all over us; and blotting out the light from the doorway was the black, hooded silhouette of the Birdman with a kittehawk perched on his shoulder.

From *Why the Whales Came* by Michael Morpurgo

Word or phrase	What it makes reader think of	What impact it has
seething and angry		

WRITING SKILLS

Summary by generalisation

Summary is the art of shortening a piece of writing whilst retaining the main meaning. One strategy for shortening is generalisation.

Generalisation is the rolling together of several points using words that cover all of them. For example:

Text	Generalisation
Tom sold not only local fruits such as apples, plums and strawberries, but he also imported fruit from around the world such as kiwis, mangoes, fresh lychees and green bananas.	Tom sold fruit.

If you were allowed six words instead of three, could you make the generalisation even closer to the original?

Check your answer on page 132.

Generalise these texts in the number of words specified:

Text	Generalisation
Dogs, cats, goldfish, hamsters, budgerigars, guinea pigs.	In 1 word
Dogs, cats, mice, guinea pigs.	In 2 words
Snakes, crocodiles, lizards, iguanas.	In 1 word
The shop sold fresh fruit and vegetables, tinned food, bread, sweets and various household items.	A full sentence of 4 words
The job includes filing, answering the telephone, taking messages, word processing and dealing with the post.	A full sentence of 5 words
Boys won five out of the seven games. The girls did better in the quiz and the table tennis, and they narrowly missed winning the art competition because Shona spilt lemonade on her painting.	A full sentence of 5 words A full sentence of 10 words

Try this exercise with a longer piece.

Activity

Try shortening this passage by generalising. Use the following starters to get you going:

Noah's sons were . . .

They ignored . . .

But they . . .

Can you do it in around 20 words?

Try doing it in 10 words.

Noah's three sons lived in different countries, took different jobs and enjoyed different lifestyles. They never contacted each other, and never communicated with their father. Even when he died, they did not attend his funeral. Yet none of them forgot their mother. One sent her baskets of rice and dried fruit every month, another wrote short letters whenever riders passed his house heading for his native land, and the other sent silver coins wrapped in palm leaves whenever the harvest was good.

(80 words)

Now try with this passage:

The customs officer gazed into Tania's suitcase and saw an array of brightly coloured skirts, sarongs and shorts. There were at least half a dozen tee-shirts in a range of acid colours and, more surprisingly, three bikinis and two swimsuits. He wasn't surprised to find the usual array of underwear, a beach towel and a sponge bag, and the four novels and five bottles of suntan lotion confirmed his first impression that Tania was heading for a holiday in the sun.

Activity

Try to summarise this passage in less than 10 words.

Try it in 15–20 words.

Compare your efforts and see if other people have found more succinct ways to generalise.

THE ART OF THE WRITER

Point of view

The point of view in a story is the perspective from which it is told: the narrative perspective. Stories can be told:

- from the inside by one of the characters speaking as 'I' (a first person narrator)

- from the outside by a narrator who seems to know everything about everybody, can tell you what people are thinking and go to any scene (an omniscient narrator)

- from the outside but following the experiences of one character.

Which of these is which?

A

Jack tossed and turned in his sleep as the nightmare gripped him, twisting his head from side to side on the pillows, until at last he woke. He looked wildly around, and then, seeing to his great relief the familiar outlines of his own safe room, fell fast asleep again.

From *The Cuckoo Child* by Dick King-Smith

B

I would watch Grandfather's experiments. I would ask him to explain what he was doing and to name the contents of his various bottles.

From *Chemistry* by Graham Swift

C

"Stop thief! Stop thief!" There is magic in the sound. The tradesman leaves his counter and the carman his wagon; the butcher throws down his tray; the baker his basket; the milkman his pail; the errand boy his parcel; the school-boy his marbles; the paviour his pack-axe; the child his battledore. Away they run, pell-mell, helter-skelter, slap-dash.

From *Oliver Twist* by Charles Dickens

In the next extract, Andrew's father has brought his boss home for a meal:

The first course is soup and bread rolls. I make loud slurping noises with the soup. No one says anything about it. I make the slurping noises longer and louder. They go on and on and on. It sounds like someone has pulled the plug out of the bath. Dad clears his throat but doesn't say anything.

The chicken is served. 'I've got the chicken's bottom,' I say in a loud voice.

Dad glares at me but he doesn't answer. I pick up the chicken and start stuffing it into my mouth with my fingers. I grab a roast potato and break it in half. I dip my fingers into the margarine and put some on the potato. It runs all over the place.

I have never seen anyone look as mad as the way Dad looks at me. He glares. He stares. He clears his throat. But still he doesn't crack. What a man. Nothing can make him break his promise.

I place the yellow fly swat on the table next to my knife.

Everyone looks at it lying there on the white table-cloth. They stare and stare and stare. But nothing is said.

I pick up the fly swat and start to lick it. I lick it like an ice cream. A bit of chewy, brown goo comes off on my tongue. I swallow it quickly. Then I crunch a bit of crispy, black stuff.

Mr Spinks rushes out to the kitchen. I can hear him being sick in the kitchen sink.

From *Licked* by Paul Jennings

Activity

1 Get into groups of four. Three of you act out the meal. Next, in turn, each of you tell the fourth person about the meal. Start:

"I've just had the most weird experience ..."

This gives you the experience of retelling the events from a different narrative perspective, but on all occasions it is still a first person perspective.

Finally, the fourth person retells the meal as an outsider saw it.

2 Go back to the extract and retell the first two paragraphs as an omniscient narrator. This means you can go inside the heads of all three characters if you need to. Although you have more freedom, it is quite hard to detach yourself from a particular character. Why is that?

3 But it's not just the events that we get from Andrew, it's also the way he tells it. In what ways is it like a sports commentary?

4 There is another person's perspective to consider and that is the reader's. What sort of reactions does the extract provoke? Read through it, stopping at the end of each paragraph to say what your reaction was at each point.

 # WRITING STYLE

A sentence to borrow: starting with time

> At midnight, when the men arrived, all the guests would stand to form a circle round the bed.

> Afterwards, fuelled by coffee and liqueur throughout the night, they would reminisce about the dead.

> And then, with some shuffling, their reminiscences would regress through the years.

Sentences taken from *Being Dead* by Jim Crace

These three sentences are, surprisingly, taken from the same page in a novel. The writer is deliberately repeating the pattern of expressions to give the sense of a routine or ritual. This is because he is describing a 'wake' in which friends sit with the body of a dead friend through the night before they are buried – an ancient ritual.

 ### Activity

What do the sentences have in common? Identify repeated patterns. Fill in the diagram, which depicts the sentences, to show:

- The main clause – the main part of the sentence.

- The bit that tells you *when*.

- The bit that tells you more about *how* and *when* the verb happened.

	,	,	.

Here are two more sentences. Add in a middle section, like an 'aside' which tells you more about how or when the verb was done. It is an *adverbial* because it adds more to the verb.

| *Later,* | | , | *they would remember the good times.* |
| *Finally,* | | , | *they would go home to their own beds.* |

Investigation: Sentence starters

The sentences opposite all start with a phrase that tells you when the events take place.

Activity

Open a novel at any page and do a survey of the first 15 sentences to see how they start.

How many start with:

- A word or phrase that is the main thing or person in the sentence?

- A phrase that tells you when, where or how something happened?

- A connecting phrase, e.g. Nevertheless?

- A verb?

Use these or any other categories to find out how good writers vary the start of their sentences.

Compare writers. They have remarkably different styles.

Now look at your own recent work in the same way. How do you tend to start your sentences? How varied are your starts?

NON-FICTION

Synthesising information 2

Your friend's family have decided to move to Australia for the year. Her father is to take a job at one of three offices in Sydney, Adelaide or Darwin. To help them decide on a city, they have listed their preferences in order. Help them to choose the place that closely matches all or most of these.

This task involves cross-referencing information about places with the family's preferences.

Mum likes:
- Shopping
- Scenic views

Sister likes:
- Animals, but has a phobia about crocodiles
- Nature, and places of natural beauty

Friend likes:
- Watersport
- Keeping cool, and not too hot

Dad likes:
- Aboriginal art
- Sightseeing

Activity

1 Read the information opposite about the three cities in Australia.

2 Decide how you will highlight the relevant information from the passages.

3 Make a grid, 4 columns wide and 5 rows deep. Write the names of the towns at the top of columns 2, 3 and 4. Write the names of the four family members in the first box of rows 2, 3, 4 and 5.

4 Complete the grid with the features that each family member will enjoy.

5 Finally, evaluate the information and choose a location that will best fit the whole family's needs.

6 Write to the family with your recommendation. Concentrate on linking your ideas together smoothly. It helps if you have ready phrases that move you from one point to the next. Use some of these phrases to help you:

I recommend that you move to …	You/your mother/father/sister would be able to …
It offers …	
You can also enjoy …	Although other cities do have …
Even better, it has …	Compared with other cities, …
For your mother/sister/father, it has …	On balance …

Sydney

Harbour and city views with shops, restaurants and many attractions can be enjoyed at Darling Harbour. Discover the spectacular Rocks, Blue Mountains, Harbour Bridge and Sydney Opera House. Take in the beautiful and inspiring views of

canyons, deep plunging valleys and lush rainforests. Visit the Australian Wildlife Park so that you can cuddle a koala. Sydney is cluttered with shops and factory outlets offering reasonably priced items. During November to March the temperature is about 27°C.

Adelaide

This place is an animal lover's paradise. Explore the redgum forest and seek out koalas sleeping in the forks of trees. Take a walk through the habitat of Kangaroo Island kangaroos, tamar wallabies and endangered glossy black cockatoos. At Seal Bay Conservation Park walk amongst Australian sea lions on a wonderful sandy beach. Buy interesting Australian items and antiques. During November to March it is warm with mild nights. It is about 27°C.

Darwin

Discover this friendly tropical city with its modern casino and popular restaurants and entertainment. Darwin has Kakadu National Park, a rich tropical region with Aboriginal rock paintings and vast landscapes – its wildlife roams free! If you take the gorge cruise you will see crocodiles sunning themselves on the banks and many other interesting species of wildlife. Darwin is a great place to buy Aboriginal art and artefacts. It is a hot and humid place with an average temperature of about 31°C.

WORD WORK

Spellings: Mathematics

First, test each other on the Geography 2 spellings from Unit 4.
Then, learn these tricky spellings for use in Mathematics lessons:

1	Sphere	**7**	Radius/radii
2	Cylinder	**8**	Diameter
3	Pyramid	**9**	Perimeter
4	Parallel	**10**	Circumference
5	Height	**11**	Ratio
6	Weight	**12**	Decimal

Puzzle

Take five minutes to think of as many words as you can using these word roots.

Can you work out what each one means?

Circ

Dec

Para

Radi

Meter

Check your answers on page 133.

Know the difference: 'Have' or 'of'?

Both words are very common, and most people spell them correctly, except in the following cases. Here are the correct versions:

Could have	**Should have**
Would have	**Might have**
Must have	**Won't have**

People get this wrong because they tend to say *could've* which sounds like *could of*.

The words *could*, *would*, *should*, etc. are called **conditional words**. This is because the actions they describe are not certain, because they are conditional upon something else.

There are more ways of making your words conditional:

Supposing …

If …

Assuming …

Might …

The word **of** is very versatile, and has several subtle meanings. Look for examples of this word in a book to find some of these meanings.

Words at work: Quantifying

The English language contains a large number of words that *quantify* meaning. In other words, they suggest to what extent it is true.

For example:

It is *quite* **wet outside.**

I am *slightly* **concerned.**

Activity

1 Make a list of six words which quantify meaning. Some of these words will help your speech and writing to sound more mature because they suggest shades of meaning. The speaker is someone who understands that the world is not always simple, and wants to keep things in perspective.

   Check your answers on page 133.

2 Make these sentences sound more considered and accurate by inserting words of quantity:

   • The ten bars of chocolate, four bags of sweeties and pork pie I ate this morning have made me feel sick.

   • I feel cross with you for leaving your slippers on the stairs.

   • Since the flood, the carpets are damp.

   • I am anxious about the effect of frost on my geraniums.

   • Neighbours are concerned about the prospect of a new motorway passing through our back gardens.

DETECTIVE READER

Using words to create atmosphere

Authors use a range of techniques to create a mood or atmosphere. Some of these techniques are listed in the left hand column. Match them to the examples in the right hand column.

Techniques:

- short sentences for impact
- appeal to the senses
- well chosen verbs
- showing not telling
- personification
- suggestive weather
- simile

His eyes were cold and steely, like a hawk's when it is about to swoop on its prey.
The tree groaned as the wind beat against its branches.
The headteacher drummed her fingers on the desk.
That stale smell hung in the air as she played with the smooth, cold metal egg the aliens had left behind. The monotone humming of the spaceship suddenly stopped and a deep silence opened up.
There was the noise again. Crackle. Snap. Somewhere behind him. But where exactly?
As he held the trophy high, his eyes began to glisten.
The steel grey clouds gathered low above the exhausted travellers and the driving rain beat down upon them.

The extract on the next page is full of suspense. The narrator is trapped in a magician's sword box on a theatre stage and Scarface is trying to kill him. Match the boxes to the effect they create in the passage.

	He snatched up one of the daggers. Maybe the dagger was fake too. But from where I was sitting, it certainly looked real.
Focus on detail	
Short sentences for impact	Slowly he advanced towards me. I had never felt more helpless. I couldn't move. I couldn't breathe. All I could do was watch. And Scarface was enjoying every second of it.
Well chosen verbs to create an image in the readers mind	He smiled at me, a smile that was full of hatred. "Wait a minute …" I began. "The first knife, ladies and gentlemen," Scarface said.
Questions to delay the outcome of the danger	He slammed it in. I shut my eyes and winced. Was I dead? Was I even wounded? I opened my eyes. Scarface looked as surprised as I did.

From *South by South East* by Anthony Horowitz

To write about these techniques, you have to describe the atmosphere and show how it has been created, with examples.

For example:

Short, panicky sentences build up the suspense, each one focused on the fear and helplessness of the narrator. It is like a slow-motion film, making the reader wait for the moment of attack.

The reader sympathises with the narrator because the story is told from his point of view, looking out of the box as Scarface bears down on him. Scarface himself is described in a menacing way. His smile is 'full of hatred' and he takes obvious enjoyment in terrifying his victim. Verbs such as 'slammed' and 'winced' conjure up images of violence and pain.

At the end, the author keeps the reader in suspense by asking questions the reader is already asking himself such as 'Was I dead?' which delays the answer and makes the reader want to know all the more.

Try it

Read the extract below in which Peter is being chased in a pitch black and empty cinema. Look out for techniques used to create suspense and write an explanation like the one above.

Something big was moving fast towards him in the darkness. He could hear the long feet beating on the carpet, the breath of it. It would be here in seconds. His nostrils were filled with the spicy, sweaty scent. Everything was so vast in the darkness and there was still no sign of the chink of light that led back to the world where everything was safe and real.

Peter found the wall. He fumbled along it looking for the door. It should have been here but it wasn't; it should be over there but it wasn't. His hand banged something down – a picture? No, it was the door frame … and there at the end of the corridor was the seam of light that led to safety.

From *The Earth Giant* by Melvin Burgess

WRITING SKILLS

Summary by deletion

Explanation

You already know that sometimes you need to shorten a text, and in Unit 4 you considered how to shorten by generalising. Another way of shortening is simply to delete the less important words. This means knowing what the main points are and keeping them in, so it is important to read the whole passage before you start deciding what to cut.

Situations in which this often happens:

1 When you trim writing to fit in a space (e.g. to fit a newspaper story in its column).

2 When it's someone else's work and you are not allowed to change the actual words (e.g. cutting down a script for a speech because it's too long).

3 When you want to cut out the hard bits so the reader can understand it (e.g. abridging a classic novel so it is easy to read).

Common deletions include:

- details
- examples
- quotations
- 'asides'
- anecdotes
- information which is repeated in different words.

Try it

What might you delete from this sentence, leaving behind a sentence of *no more than 15 words* that still makes sense?

> All things considered, Angel felt he liked Buffy, but she wasn't as important to him as she liked to think, and so he decided to leave her for a starring role in a new series.

Compare your answer with that on page 133.

Here is a paragraph from *A Day in the Life of a Roman Centurian*. Edit it down to *no more than 30 words*. First read it and decide what is the most important information. Then decide what you can cut out without spoiling the meaning.

> Life was lonely for the commander's children. They were not allowed to play outside the camp with native children, who did not even speak Latin. Neither sons nor daughters went to school. Instead they took lessons from private tutors. Children learnt Latin and Greek by writing with a pointed stylus on a wax tablet. Lessons were hard, and some girls must have longed for their twelfth birthday – when they could marry.
>
> (71 words)

Compare your answer with that on page 133.

Flow

When you delete words, you have to pay attention to the joins between the bits left in. The text still has to flow. Go back to your last edit and join the sentences so they flow.

You may:

- make small changes to the wording

- add new words to link sentences together

- move the position of words so they flow.

But you must also:

- keep as close as possible to the original style and content

- not exceed 30 words.

Compare your answer with that on page 133.

THE ART OF THE WRITER

Setting

Stories are set in time and place. Scenes in a story shift from one place to another, and sometimes from one time to another. Setting includes:

- historical period
- time of day
- geographical location
- environment
- weather or climate.

The setting is important because:

- A description of a new setting can help to move the reader from one scene to another (e.g. at home, at work).
- It sets the mood or atmosphere (e.g. raging storm).
- It gives you clues about the characters who live there (e.g. character's living room).
- It can signal the kind of story (e.g. spooky old house).

Sometimes settings are central to the story. Think of stories and novels that mention a setting in the title, such as:

The Railway Children
The Secret Garden

Try it

- Here is an extract. Find as many clues as you can about where and when it takes place.

> I pedal furiously now, not because I want to catch up with them but because this road is deserted and I want to reach a better road or highway as soon as possible. I feel more vulnerable than ever. There are no houses in sight. Most of the cars use the Interstate that runs parallel to this old road. I keep pedalling. There's a curve ahead. Maybe there'll be a house or a new road or something around the curve.
>
> I hear the car again. That unmistakable motor. The car is coming back. The car is rounding the curve, heading in my direction. The car's grille looks like a grinning mouth of some metal monster.

From *I Am the Cheese* by Robert Cormier

Here are three more extracts. Work out for each one where and when you think it may be set.

A

It was a summer of sudden thunder. The first storm came one Wednesday in July. Hot! It was the sort of day when the earth cracks, dogs run mad and even friends are best avoided. The sky which only half an hour ago had been a dry blue, now thickened with dark clouds. Soon it was going to rain very hard and anyone caught far from shelter would be soaked to the skin.

From *The Stonewalkers* by Vivien Alcock

B

When Chas awakened, the air-raid shelter was silent. Grey winter light was creeping round the door-curtain. It could have been anytime. His mother was gone, and the little brown attaché case with the insurance policies and bottle of brandy for emergencies. He could hear the milk-cart coming round the square. The all-clear must have gone.

From *The Machine Gunners* by Robert Westall

C

Potts arrived with his keys jiggling in his hand and an expression that was both cruel and smug smeared across his face. Maddie was frog-marched out of the room and along the basement corridor. Potts pulled back the grate on the spy hole in the cell door. He peered in, then grunted. The key was turned in the lock. Maddie was shoved into the cell and the door slammed behind her. The lock turned with a harsh metallic squeal and echoing footsteps receded into the distance.
Maddie stood in the harsh light from the single unshaded bulb that hung from the ceiling. She stood and stared at the man sitting on the edge of the bed.

From *The Memory Prisoner* by Thomas Bloor

Activity

Match these statements to the extracts:

1 The sentences that describe the setting become more complex in structure, building up a feeling that something bad is going to happen.

2 The setting is described to make it sound seedy and unsettling.

3 The setting is described through someone else's eyes.

4 The setting moves from being silent to including sounds.

5 There is a sense of cruelty in the language used to describe the setting.

6 The character is not familiar with the setting.

7 The vital information is written in the shortest sentences.

We often think of settings as descriptions of things. However, it is more often the verbs that do the hard work. Find the most powerful verb in each extract, and explain how it helps to set the scene.

WRITING STYLE

A sentence to borrow: animating verbs

Read the sentence below:

> I peered in my box of toys and saw the white, clean bones of a small creature that had died in there.

What is interesting about this sentence is that it repeats the basic action using different words:

I peered

I saw

It is really two sentences joined by the word *and*. The effect is to stretch time out and give special shock value to what he sees. This is because it keeps the reader waiting, wanting to know what the narrator saw.

Another interesting thing is that it uses only very simple words. Only one word is longer than one syllable. It sounds very childlike and innocent, which is odd when you consider what it describes. It makes the reader anxious for the child narrator.

Activity

Try writing another sentence in which the boy continues his search in the garage, using these words:

I touched .... *and felt* ....

I glimpsed .... *and saw* ....

I sensed .... *and knew* ....

Remember to keep it simple, and to put your shocks into the second part.

Can you think of other pairs of verbs that could be used for similar sentences?

Taking on a life of its own

It's no surprise that most verbs are 'performed' by animate objects. But writers can easily put verbs with inanimate objects for effect. For example:

The car <u>swerved</u> across the road.

The implication is that it is out of human control.

The cliff <u>towered</u> above us.

The implication is that humans feel overawed by the sight.

An *animate* object is a living thing such as a person or an animal, that can think and move for itself.

An *inanimate* object is not a living thing. It can't think and it can't move by itself.

What is the implication of:

The ball <u>rocketed</u> towards him.

The mirror <u>mocked</u> him.

The ship <u>heaved</u> and <u>sighed</u> in the waves.

Now look back at Extract C on page 65, and pick out the verbs that relate to inanimate objects. There are quite a few. What effect is the writer trying to create by giving life to inanimate objects?

Imagine yourself afraid as you grope your way through a dark place, and write a paragraph in which shadowy inanimate objects seem to gain a life of their own, by giving them verbs.

NON-FICTION

Lay-out

Here are a number of extracts about child labour in the 19th century.
Notice how different the texts look.

A

No. 72 –Mary Barrett, aged 14.   *June 15.*
I have worked down in pit five years; father is working in next pit; I have 12 brothers and sisters … one of them can read, none of the rest can, or write; they never went to day–school, but three of them go to Sunday-school; I hurry for my brother John, and come down at seven o'clock about; I go up at six, sometimes seven; I do not like working in pit, but I am obliged to get a living; I work always without stockings, or shoes, or trousers; I wear nothing but my chemise; I have to go up to the headings with the men; they are all naked there; I am got well used to that, and don't care now much about it; I was afraid at first, and did not like it; they never behave rudely to me; I cannot read or write.

B

1881 British Census

	Marr.	Age	Sex	Birthplace
Willm. J. ROBERTS	U	12	M	Reigate, Surrey, England

Rel: Serv

Occ: Page

C

1832	1833	1842	1864	1870
Investigation by parliament into conditions in the textile factories.	Slavery abolished in British Empire. Act passed to limit working hours for women and children in textile work.	Investigation into working conditions in mines. Act passed to ban the use of boys under 13 and all women and girls in mines.	Campaign led to the passing of an act making it illegal for boys to be used as chimney sweeps.	Education Act made it compulsory for all children between the ages of 5 and 10 to be educated.

D *Girl pulling a coal tub in mine &*
1871 Child making matchboxes

E Poor Children at Work

Jobs in coal mines
Work in textile mills and factories
Domestic servants
Match makers and sellers
Chimney sweeps
Street sellers
Bone collectors and sorters

Activity

Describe for each extract:

- the type of text

- the purpose of the text

- the lay-out and why it is appropriate.

Example

Source A is a first hand recount by a Victorian teenager. It was probably written as evidence of real-life conditions in the mines. It is written in the first person and although it might be a transcript of an interview, it has been recorded in prose so that the evidence of the girl's account is preserved, and not interpreted in someone else's words.

Now do the same for sources B–E.

Now answer these questions:

1 Which texts include only provable facts?

2 What questions would you want to ask about each text to be sure it was honest and accurate?

3 Which texts would you use if you wanted to persuade someone that child labour was a terrible thing?

WORD WORK

Spellings: RE

First test each other on the Mathematics spellings from Unit 5.
Then, learn these tricky spellings for use in RE:

1 Religion/religious
2 Pray/prayer
3 Christianity
4 Symbol
5 Neighbour
6 Creator
7 Disciple
8 Preach
9 Marriage
10 Baptism
11 Hymn
12 Believe
13 Prophet

"No you fool, I said let's celebrate the prophets!"

Puzzle

- Identify four of the words in the list above that are homophones.
  They have counterparts which sound identical but are spelt differently. What are the meanings of the other words and how do you spell them?

  Check your answers on page 133.

- For fun, try pronouncing these words in different ways so that their silent letters can be heard. This is a good strategy for remembering the shy letters.

Know the difference

Take another three minutes to race each other to list triple homophones.

For example:

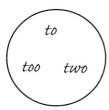

Find answers on page 133.

Words at work: Adverbs

'LY' words are adverbs, because they add something to the verb.

Try starting a sentence with an adverb. For example:

Sensibly, Sam soon stopped worrying and slipped into sleep.

Cautiously, she peered around the corner and saw the men disappear into a doorway.

Quickly, Maria grabbed the gun from the dead man's hand and pointed it at the door.

The adverb comes before the main sentence opens. It sets the tone but makes the reader wait to hear what it's all about. It focuses the reader on the *how* rather than the *what*.

Notice the comma which separates the adverb from the main clause. The comma is usually followed by the person or subject of the sentence, e.g. Maria, Sam.

Examples of adverbs
Slowly
Thoughtfully
Luckily
Reluctantly
Hesitantly
Patiently
Quickly

Activity

Try writing three sentences about a chase starting:

Quickly . . .

Instantly . . .

Cruelly . . .

DETECTIVE READER

Developing an impression

Good readers 'grow' their impressions about characters and events in a book. At first, they pick up clues to gain an impression of the characters and events, and look for evidence to support or adjust those impressions.

Example

In this extract, you soon latch on to the fact that Gwyn's grandmother is upset, because:

A She uses sarcasm

B She avoids eye contact

C She tells him why she is upset

D Her tone is unfriendly

E She treats him like an intruder

Examples have been picked out in the text. Which statement goes in which box?

> Gwyn started, then smiled. It was too late to run away. <u>She didn't speak, didn't move</u>.
>
> "Hullo, Nain!" he said at last and his voice sounded withered and unwilling.
>
> <u>His grandmother looked away from him.</u> She was holding a trowel which she began to poke into the dry soil. <u>When she spoke she seemed to be addressing the earth.</u> <u>"Snooping are we Gwydion Gwyn?"</u> she said.
>
> "No, not snooping, Nain," he said.
>
> <u>"Why didn't you come to the door, then, instead of lurking in my ground like a thief?"</u>
>
> "I wasn't lurking, Nain. I was just passing," he said huffily. He felt silly peering through the sprays of coloured leaves.
>
> "I see. <u>Not coming to see *me*, then!"</u>
>
> "Well…" he shifted from one foot to the other.
>
> <u>"So run along, then," she said coldly.</u> <u>"Don't let me detain you from your urgent business."</u>
>
> All at once Gwyn felt that he should speak to his grandmother.

From *The Chestnut Soldier* by Jenny Nimmo

Activity

To write up an analysis of these points, you should:

1 State your overall impression of grandmother's feelings.

2 Justify your impression by making the five points you have gathered. Aim to spend five sentences on this – one on each point.

3 As you go through the five points, prove them by providing examples or quotations from the extract.

4 Finish by saying what the overall effect is.

Try this and then check your attempt with the one on page 134.

Try it

Read the passage below in which Cameron, who is very ill, has decided with the help of his father to undergo a dangerous operation to save his life.

I glanced at my alarm clock. It was 1.30 in the morning. Mum and Dad would be fast asleep by now. Feeling for my slippers, I put them on and tiptoed to the door and out of my room. Gingerly, I crept down the stairs. A sudden, unexpected sound from the front room froze me in my tracks. There it was again. Dad couldn't still be there. The light was off. But… it sounded a bit like Dad. What was going on? Why on earth was Dad sitting in the dark? I tiptoed to the closed front-room door. What should I do? Now I was at the door, I could see just the faintest light seeping out from the room. Dad must have switched on his anglepoise lamp rather than the main light. Very gently, I opened the door.

It was Dad. He sat at his table with his back towards the door.

"Dad?" I whispered.

Dad's head whipped round at the sound of my voice. I stared, profoundly shocked. I saw something I'd never, ever seen in my life. Something I never thought I'd see.

Dad was crying.

"Dad?" I didn't know what else to say.

Embarrassed, Dad quickly wiped his eyes.

"Dad, are you OK?"

"I'm fine."

I inwardly grimaced. A stupid question followed by a blatant lie.

"Go on Cameron. Off you go to bed," Dad said firmly.

I wanted to stay. I desperately wanted to stay. I wanted to sit down and talk to Dad and say … things. But instead I nodded and backed out of the room, closing the door carefully behind me.

From *Pig-Heart Boy* by Malorie Blackman

Activity

How does the writer let us know what Cameron's Dad is thinking and feeling in this extract? Try picking out the main points, then writing it up in a paragraph with examples to justify your views.

WRITING SKILLS

Short and sweet

In previous units you have learnt that you can shorten text without losing the main points by:

- Cutting out the less important points.

- Generalising.

- Joining up the remaining sections to allow the text to flow.

Grant doesn't know this! He left the following note for his mum:

> Dear Mum
>
> I have decided to go over to Darren's house to see if he fancies watching a video. I will probably stay at his house for the afternoon and come home for my tea. I will probably be back home at about 5.30 this afternoon. So I will see you then. I hope the shopping went well.
>
> Lots of love,
>
> From Grant

- Reduce the note to no more than eight words by editing out unnecessary information.

Grant's Mum is just as bad. Here is the note she left him a little later:

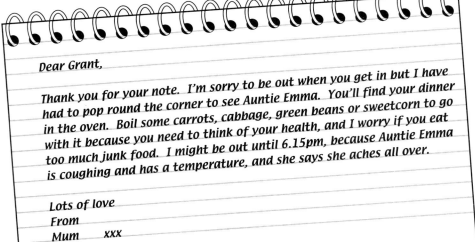

> Dear Grant,
>
> Thank you for your note. I'm sorry to be out when you get in but I have had to pop round the corner to see Auntie Emma. You'll find your dinner in the oven. Boil some carrots, cabbage, green beans or sweetcorn to go with it because you need to think of your health, and I worry if you eat too much junk food. I might be out until 6.15pm, because Auntie Emma is coughing and has a temperature, and she says she aches all over.
>
> Lots of love
> From
> Mum   xxx

● Rewrite the note from Grant's Mum so it fits comfortably on a Post-it note. Edit out *and* generalise to do this.

Grant's brother (Darren) has also left a post it note which worries both Grant and his Mum when they read it:

Gone sleepover.

Back soon.

D.

● Explain why this note is bound to worry the family, and what Darren should have written.

Here is another of Darren's attempts at note-making. He made these notes in Science over a month ago so that he could revise for his exam next week. How useful will they be?

Contracting means getting shorter. Stretched by other muscles. Impulses = messages from nervous system. Food. 1. Bones – moves body when you want it. Voluntary. Bends skeleton at joints. 2. Contract when you don't think about it. Pushes food along gut. 3. Around heart. Not tired for years. Insects and birds have muscles around wings. Shellfish contract muscles and don't get tired for hours on end.

Darren is quite clever. At the time, he understood what he was reading, but he recorded it very badly. What is wrong with his notes and how could he improve them?

When you have done this, make your own version of notes. Compare them with other people's and decide what makes good notes.

THE ART OF THE WRITER

Mood

Mood is the emotional feel of a passage. It often arises from the mood of the narrator. It is harder to spot than atmosphere because it is usually communicated in the way a story is told rather than through the things it describes.

Examples of moods are:

Thoughtful	Sombre
Playful	Optimistic
Remorseful	

Here is a writer thinking back to something that once happened to him:

A snake came to my water-trough
On a hot, hot day, and I in my pyjamas for the heat,
To drink there.

In the deep, strange-scented shade of the great dark carob-tree
I came down the steps with my pitcher
And must wait, must stand and wait, for there he was at the trough before me.
He reached down from a fissure in the earth-wall in the gloom
And trailed his yellow-brown slackness soft-bellied down, over the edge of the stone trough
And rested his throat upon the stone bottom,
And where the water had dripped from the tap, in a small clearness,
He sipped with his straight mouth,
Softly drank through his straight gums, into his slack long body,
Silently …

… He drank enough
And lifted his head, dreamily, as one who has drunken,
And flickered his tongue like a forked light on the air, so black,
Seeming to lick his lips,
And looked around like a god, unseeing, into the air,
And slowly turned his head,
And slowly, very slowly, as if thrice adream,
Proceeded to draw his slow length curving round
And climb again the broken bank of my wall-face …

… I looked round, I put down my pitcher,
I picked up a clumsy log
And threw it at the water-trough with a clatter.

From *Snake* by D.H. Lawrence

Activity

The mood is *listless* because it is hot. This is the feeling you get when it is so hot that you can't be bothered to exert yourself. Here is how the writer has achieved this mood. Find examples of the following techniques in the poem.

1 Words repeated to emphasise how hot and close it feels.

2 Words repeated to emphasise how slow and heavy everything is.

3 Words used which suggest how detached the writer feels from events.

4 Alliteration used to suggest the hissing of the heat and of the snake.

5 Repeated use of long vowels to slow down the words.

6 Sentence links which suggest how hard it is for the writer to think and link ideas. It is too hot to think.

- The mood of the writer is also *contemplative* which means he is in a thoughtful or reflective mood, thinking over a past event. Can you pick out some ways in which the poet has communicated his contemplative mood?

- Choose a different mood for the same scene (e.g. excited, frightened) and write a few lines of verse mirroring your mood.

 # WRITING STYLE

A sentence to borrow: commas

Here are three sentences from the same novel. Can you see what they have in common?

> He laughed, not cynically but with evident humour.

> She tried to think of a way of outflanking him, of getting the information she desperately needed.

> Rachel jumped to her feet, too restless to remain at her desk.

From *Please Come Home* by Michael Hardcastle

There are clearly two parts to each sentence – one before and one after the comma. The first part is the main clause. You know this because it would make sense on its own. The second part goes on to 'unpack' the first by providing more particular information.

The comma in these sentences is almost acting like an abbreviation for words which have been omitted (shown in italics below).

For example:

> **He laughed,** *but he was* **not** *laughing* **cynically but with evident humour.**

Note that the italicised words do not appear in the original sentence. This is a trick we use a lot in speaking, and it is becoming more common in writing. It has evolved as a way of saving words. You can see here that it cuts out the repetition of the word *laugh*.

● Which words are omitted but implied in the other two sentences?

Writers sometimes uses this device when they write an extended sentence, as a way of dropping in extra detail as an 'aside'. For example:

> **Rachel jumped to her feet, too restless to remain at her desk,** *and bounded for the door.*

Activity

- Extend the original sentence beginning 'She tried to think...'

- Now write three sentences using the same structure. You could start:

The dog sprang up . . .

Jake lunged for the rope . . .

Mother brushed her hair thoughtfully . . .

Investigation: Commas

Open a modern novel at any page and look for sentences that contain commas. Ignore the ones that use commas in lists, and the ones that sit between speech and sentence. Just look at the ones that use commas to chunk up the sentence.

Find the main clause in each sentence: the important bit that makes sense on it own, and tells you who did what. The comma usually acts as a buffer between the main clause and the rest of the sentence.

Look at the other bits on the other side of the comma. How do they relate to the main clause? They very often give the who, how, when and where of the main clause.

Find a much older novel by Charles Dickens, Jane Austen or Charlotte Brontë and compare the length of sentences and the use of commas. What do you notice?

NON-FICTION

Describing non-fiction texts

You are used to describing the way fiction and poetry work. You can talk about plot, chapters, verses, rhythm, rhyme, alliteration and so on. You also need to be able to describe the way non-fiction texts work in three ways:

> **Text level** – how the text is organised and sequenced.
>
> **Sentence level** – how the text is expressed.
>
> **Word level** – what sort of words are used.

There are six main types of non-fiction text:

Recount	tells events in the order in which they happened
Instructions	tell you how to do something
Information	tells you about facts
Explanation	explains how things work or develop
Persuasion	puts forward an opinion or urges an idea
Discursive writing	discusses ideas and opinions

Draw a grid with these titles and four extra columns like this:

Text	2 examples	Text level	Sentence level	Word level
Recount				
Instructions				
Information				
Explanation				
Persuasion				
Discursive writing				

Here are 12 examples, two for each type of text. Which go with which? Put two letters against each type of text in the 'Examples' column.

A A recipe

B An election manifesto

C An essay about the causes of the First World War

D A report of a school trip

E An entry in an encyclopaedia

F An advertisement

G An article about a celebrity in a magazine

H A page explaining the rain cycle

I A repair manual

J A match report

K A telephone directory

L A page explaining how a jet engine works

Here are six **TEXT LEVEL** features. Which goes with which text type? Put the correct letter in the text column of the grid:

A Organised to emphasise cause and effect. Chunked up into stages of the process, often with helpful diagrams.

B Organised in order of event, step by step, very clear and concise, often in numbered points.

C Organised to have immediate impact and appeal. Most important and attention-grabbing points first.

D Organised in paragraphs to lead the reader through the points, balancing different points of view as it goes.

E Organised by order of event, but stopping to dwell on interesting points and issues.

F Organised by topic, with sub-headings and often with helpful illustrations.

Here are six **SENTENCE LEVEL** features. Which goes with which type of text? Put the correct letter in the sentence column:

A Written as commands. Short, direct sentences.

B Often written as I or We. Many links which stress time and sequence, e.g. So then we …

C Formal expression. Very clear. Often in present tense. Many links emphasise cause and effect, e.g. resulting in …

D Formal expression. Third person. Often in present tense. Many statements of fact, no opinions.

E Mix of fact, interviews, quotations. Mainly present tense unless reporting a real-life event. Balancing phrase, e.g. on the other hand, though others claim.

F Often short, even catchy sentences to catch the attention. Sometimes commands for the same reason. Assertive, and makes frequent appeals to reader by posing questions, e.g. Doesn't it make sense to …?

And here are six **WORD LEVEL** features. Which goes with which type of text? Put the correct letter in the word column:

A Attention-grabbing words to catch the interest or even to shock, e.g. new, big, better, crisis, vandal, boss, terrorist.

B Words sometimes refer to feelings and reflection, e.g. we felt, looking back, it seemed so.

C Commanding verbs. Plain words, very clear and direct. No description or imagery. Occasional technical vocabulary.

D Many words of qualification, e.g. even though, although, sometimes, not forgetting, occasionally and words which link and weigh ideas, e.g. therefore, on the whole, equally.

E Formal, clear, often precise and unemotional vocabulary. Technical vocabulary introduced and used.

F Plain vocabulary, very clear, emphasis on link words. Technical vocabulary often introduced and used.

Check your answers on page 134.

Find examples of non-fiction writing in your classroom and decide what text type they fall into, or if it is a text book, what different text types it contains.

Continue this activity in the next unit.

WORD WORK

Spellings: Art, Design and Technology

First test each other on the RE spellings from Unit 6. Then, learn these tricky spellings to use in Art, Design and Technology:

1 Design

2 Technology

3 Horizontal

4 Vertical

5 Diagonal

6 Texture

7 Perspective

8 Dimension

9 Alternative

10 Machine

11 Engine

12 Research

Puzzle

Arrange the words in a list so that each word shares at least two consecutive letters with the word above. There is a way to list all 12, e.g.

diago**nal**

vertical

alternat**ive**

Check your answer on page 134.

Know the difference: Plural apostrophes

The apostrophe usually comes before the 'S'.

But it comes after the 'S' if the word is plural.

For example:

The boy's coats (one boy with lots of coats)

The boys' coats (several boys)

 HELP

Pronouns don't use an apostrophe, even when they show possession

For example:

Yours

Hers

Activity

What do these mean?

- The ladies' coats.

- The dog's lead.

- The teacher's pet.

- The teachers' books.

When you say these words, you can't see or hear the apostophe. How, then, do you know what the speaker means?

Can you explain:

- What **it's** means?

- What **its** means?

- Why there is no such word as **its'**?

Check your answers on page 135.

Words at work: Specificity

Specificity is the degree to which a word is exactly right for describing what you mean.

For example:

Animal is very general.

Dog is more specific.

Labrador is even more specific.

Said is a very general verb.

Complained is a more specific verb.

Whined is an even more specific verb.

Try making the following sentences more specific by changing words, but not moving them and not adding to them.

> **'Why not?' asked the boy in a cross way.**

> **With a big bang, the planet Zoton exploded into lots of little pieces.**

Now look at your own recent work and find places where your work could be improved by making words more specific.

DETECTIVE READER

Reading between the lines

Authors deliberately leave out details in a story. They leave gaps for the reader to fill with their imagination. The reader fills these gaps by:

- using clues which the author has left for the reader to find

- bringing their own ideas, knowledge and memories to the story.

- working out what would be likely and 'fit' in the story.

Example

In the extract below, the reader is tempted to guess what happened to the man in the photograph:

Grandma pulled out a locket from her desk drawer. Inside was a black and white portrait of a young man in khaki and a lock of straw coloured hair.

"My grandfather?" I asked softly.

Grandma's lips moved but no sound came out. At first she stared into the face of the young man, smiling, and then her right forefinger brushed the corner of her eye and she turned her head away. I reached for her shaking shoulder and left my hand there in the silence that followed.

The young man may have died in the war because khaki is the colour of uniforms

Grandma may be crying because she loved the man in the portrait. At first she is probably remembering the happiness she had and then she feels sad that he is not there anymore.

You may have had a different interpretation of Grandma's behaviour. The man might have been her brother. Perhaps he is in prison. Different people bring different ideas to a passage and understand it in different ways. So, whatever your answer, make sure you justify it and explain how you work it out.

Try it

Answer each question and justify your answer:

A What sort of life do the owners of this cottage lead? How do you know?

> The floor was trodden earth but two dirty sacks had been laid in front of the fire as a makeshift carpet. On a shelf in the wall by the fire stood two onions, placed as if they were precious objects. On the rough wooden table, which was the only proper furniture in the room, together with the bench which stood by it, was half a loaf of dark grainy bread and an earthenware pot with a knife stuck in it.

From *The Stove Haunting* by Bel Mooney

B Why does grandmother laugh? How do you know?

> Grandmother continued with her fairy story to the end where the King said ... "Let this be a lesson to us, Hannah my dear, not to overlook a treasure that is under our noses simply because we are used to it. Rachel my dear, we would be honoured if you would consider marrying our son."
>
> "So did they marry and live happily ever after?" I asked. My Grandmother laughed. "They married. Ever after I don't know about, but what I do know ..."

From *My Grandmother's Stories* by Adele Geras

C How does the Czar feel when his advisers return with the answer to a riddle he has set to catch them out? How do you know?

> The trouble only began when they came to the Czar and told him the answer.
>
> "How can you possibly know this?" shouted the Czar.
>
> "We met a Jewish farmer called Frankel on the road," they said, "and he told us."
>
> "And he undertook to say nothing, the scoundrel!" The Czar stamped his foot and sent for his Chief of Police.

From *My Grandmother's Stories* by Adele Geras

D What sort of person is Sarah? How do you know?

> The sheep made Sarah smile. She sank her fingers into their thick, coarse wool. She talked to them, running with the lambs, letting them suck on her fingers. She named them after her favourite aunts, Harriet and Mattie and Lou. She lay down in the field beside them and sang "Summer Is Icumen in," her voice drifting over the meadow grasses, carried by the wind.
>
> She cried when we found a lamb that had died, and she shouted and shook her fist at the Turkey Buzzards that came from nowhere to eat it. She would not let Caleb or me come near. And that night, Papa went with a shovel to bury the sheep and a lantern to bring Sarah back. She sat on the porch alone. Nick crept up to lean against her knees.

From *Sarah Plain and Tall* by Patricia MacLachlan

WRITING SKILLS

Developing paragraphs

You have seen that paragraphs help the writer to organise the material, and help the reader to follow it. You also know how useful the first sentence can be in focusing the reader's attention. But that's not the end of it. The rest of the paragraph is organised, too, and needs signposting.

A paragraph can go on to:

- explain the main point in more detail

- illustrate the main point with an example or quotation

- provide facts or evidence

- describe what happens next

- add information.

Here are three paragraphs. How do they build on the main point?

A Leather is made from the hide of dead animals. First, the skin is cured in salt to preserve it, then soaked in water to clean it. Chemicals are used to clean and soften the hide, so that the hairs and fur can be scraped away. Next it is dyed, and finally waterproofed using oil or wax.

B Secondary pupils are more prone to backache than they were twenty years ago. One reason is the heavy weight of books they are expected to carry from lesson to lesson. A typical pupil in Year 7 carries between 5–10 books each day. The habit of carrying bags casually over one shoulder is another factor contributing to backache problems, the experts claim. The weight of the bag curves the spine and strains the back muscles. Further damage is done if pupils walk long distances with heavy packs. In the past, teachers came to pupils' own classrooms, but today pupils are expected to move around to the teacher's classroom. Unfortunately, backache problems do not always emerge until later in life when it is too late.

C A local man surprised his neighbours yesterday by planting plastic flowers in front gardens along his street. The flowers appeared overnight last Friday. Colin Tubb of Greeve in Yorkshire said he had done it to celebrate his engagement to Julie Threadneedle. 'I was overjoyed when Julie said yes,' he told reporters. 'I wanted everyone to share my happiness.' Mr Tubb has promised to 'pick' the flowers next weekend and present them to his fiancée.

Activity

- Find **four** words in **Paragraph A** that guide the reader through the stages of the process, to remind the reader that the events are explained in order.

- Find **three** places where the writer of **Paragraph B** reminds the reader that she is listing the causes of backache.

- **Paragraph C** is a news story but it is not told in the order in which it happened. What has determined the order of the sentences?

Closing paragraphs

If opening sentences provide important signs for the reader, so do closing sentences. Closing sentences can:

- sum up the paragraph

- draw a conclusion

- round off

- signal that the paragraph is ending

- prepare the reader for the next paragraph.

Which three of the six sentences below are opening sentences, and which three are closing sentences? Work out which is which and how you know.

A Finally, remove the protective wrapper and turn the table the right way up.

B The arrival of Aunt May was a turning point for the family.

C But she never asked again.

D It was too much, and much too late.

E Next day, Rashid woke early and rode over to the harbour ready for the first catch.

F Koalas sleep for eighteen hours every day and are mainly active in the evening.

Finally, study the final sentences of Paragraphs A, B and C on the opposite page and work out how they signal the close of the paragraph.

THE ART OF THE WRITER

Character

We know characters through:

1 behaviour – what they say and do, and how they relate to other characters

2 appearance

3 belongings (e.g. if their homes are described)

4 their inner thoughts and feelings, if we are told them

5 associations with similar characters (e.g. stereotypes)

6 the attitude of the narrator to them, especially if it is a first person narrator.

But we also have to bear in mind:

● the narrator may be biased

● the writer may be keeping the true character of the person hidden

● characters develop and change.

Can you think of examples of stories in which:

● The writer conceals the true character of someone (e.g. the villain in a murder mystery)?

● A character has a striking appearance?

● A character is a stereotype?

● A character has a distinctive way of speaking?

● A character's personality is revealed by their surroundings (e.g their workplace or home)?

● A character's name hints at their personality?

Read the extract opposite from *Great Expectations* by Charles Dickens. Pip meets a man in the graveyard. What do you learn about the character of this 'fearful man'?

'Hold your noise!' cried a terrible voice, as a man started up from among the graves at the side of the church porch. 'Keep still, you little devil, or I'll cut your throat!'

A fearful man, all in coarse grey, with a great iron on his leg. A man with no hat, and with broken shoes, and with an old rag tied round his head. A man who had been soaked in water, and smothered in mud, and lamed by stones, and cut by flints, and stung by nettles, and torn by briars; who limped and shivered, and glared and growled; and whose teeth chattered in his head as he seized me by the chin …

The man, after looking at me for a moment, turned me upside down, and emptied my pockets. There was nothing in them but a piece of bread. When the church came to itself – for he was so sudden and strong that he made it go head over heels before me, and I saw the steeple under my feet – when the church came to itself, I say, I was seated on a high tombstone, trembling, while he ate the bread ravenously.

Activity

- Go through the six ways a writer paints character in the first list opposite and see how many are used by Dickens to convey information about this man.

- Some things Dickens tells us, and some things we work out for ourselves. In this case, you should have worked out that the man is an escaped prisoner. Go back and find at least three clues. Check your answers on page 135.

- Dickens has a good reason for leaving us to work it out for ourselves. What is it? Check your answer on page 135.

- How would you expect this character to behave in the rest of the book? Explain your answer. How much of it depends on prejudice and stereotype? If you know the story, you will realise that Dickens is cleverly misleading the reader about the man's true character.

Now try writing a paragraph or two without a title describing a character from the point of view of a child, so that your reader can work out more of the character than the narrator. For example:

- a child greeted by a long-lost aunt

- a first visit to a doctor or dentist

- an accidental meeting with someone very famous (but the narrator doesn't know it!).

Swap or read aloud paragraphs to see if you can guess each other's character.

WRITING STYLE

A sentence to borrow: semi-colons

> Air razored my throat; my lungs felt as if they were bleeding.

> I would find the right boy; he would see that I was the right girl.

> My mother had applied a home perm; the curls were still coiled tight.

Sentences taken from *Once in a House on Fire* by Andrea Ashworth

Each of these three sentences uses a **semi-colon** to join together two short clauses. Each clause could be a sentence on its own.

Why has the writer chosen to hitch them together with a semi-colon?

● It alerts the reader to the closeness of the two halves, and suggests that the two ideas are inseparable.

● It leaves it with the reader to make the connection between the two halves. The writer could have used a word to join the two halves (*and* or *moreover* would have done) but has chosen the semi-colon to force the reader to make the link.

● It tells you that the connection is so obvious to the narrator that it doesn't have to be explained to the reader. In the second example, it warns you that the narrator is full of romantic ideals because she naively expects to be loved back by the man of her dreams.

● The closeness of the two halves is often reinforced by a 'mirror' effect in which a pattern, word or meaning from one half is reflected in the other.

In the first example, the mirror image is created by the link between the word *razor* and *bleeding.* Both halves describe the physical pain of breathing.

Activity

- Explain how the mirror images are created in the other two examples.

- Try writing the other half of these sentences:

  The first signs of daylight appeared;......

  ......; I would leave within three months.

- Write two sentences of your own in which two inseparable short sentences are joined.

Using short sentences

Short sentences have impact. They are pithy and direct. A short sentence coming at the end of longer sentences has a special force.

Here is a paragraph containing five sentences. Look for the punctuation and length of sentences. What do you notice?

> Drained by phone calls, our mother grew thinner and thinner, until the bones pressed against the skin on her face and jutted across her chest. Her shoulders sagged, her feet dragged. She stopped picking up the phone. She stopped dressing us for school. She stopped getting out of bed.

From *Once in a House on Fire* by Andrea Ashworth

Activity

- Try reading the paragraph aloud to hear the effect of the sentences. They communicate the mental condition of the mother, who is having a breakdown. How?

- Find two other techniques used by the writer to communicate the breakdown.

- Write a paragraph in which the sentences get shorter to describe someone who is exhausted with running. Start:
  My lungs were bursting and I could hardly catch my breath ....

- Write a paragraph in which the sentences get longer to describe someone falling asleep. Start:
  As she sat there, her eyes became fixed on a corner of the room, and her breathing slowed ...

NON-FICTION

The art of persuasion

Some texts set out to persuade the reader to think or do something.
The aim is to prompt the reader into action. For example:

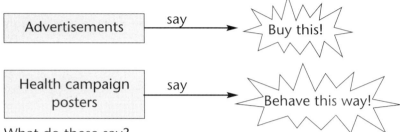

What do these say?

- holiday brochures
- charity leaflets
- film trailers

- election manifestoes
- wayside pulpits – religious posters outside churches

To persuade in words, writers can use a range of techniques. Match the technique to a sentence from this advertisement for a holiday resort:

A Exaggeration	**1** Have you ever wanted to come face to face with a shark?
B Invitation to think positively	**2** Set in the midst of some of the most stunning countryside this country has to offer, Cormer Castle echoes with the sound of the past.
C Assertion – a point of view expressed as fact	**3** Come to Cormer – England at its best.
D Use of appealing descriptive language	**4** And this year, we introduce Cormercard – 33% off every attraction for the entire summer!
	5 Soft Spring sunshine and warming sea breezes caress the coast.
E Addressing the reader directly	**6** You can choose from a wide range of wonderful restaurants.
F Appeal to the senses	**7** Cormer is a favourite with families, such as the McIntyres. "We wouldn't go anywhere else!" say the McIntyres.
G Appeal to the head	**8** The loveliest garden in the world.
H Appeal to the heart	**9** Fall in love all over again with beautiful Britain.
I Command	**10** Two out of every three visitors return the following year – it's a fact!
J Hard evidence (e.g. statistics)	**11** So affordable and easy to reach, right here in England.
K Soft evidence (e.g. opinion)	**12** Out of this world, beyond your imagination!
L Incentive (e.g. rewards, money off)	

Formula One Experience

www.tangerineuk.cor

You can feel the adrenalin rush just thinking about it. Imagine driving an Ex-Grand Prix Formula One Racing Car - a monster with a power to weight ratio 6 times greater than that of a Porsche 911, capable of speeds of 200mph and reaching 60mph quicker than it has taken you to read the last five words. The noise is almost deafening. The cars are powered by Judd V10/Cosworth V8 engines, capable of producing more than 600bhp. Just climbing into the driving seat will send tingles down your spine. Today that childhood dream has become a reality... you're not just going to watch Formula One... you're going to drive one!

Activity

1 Now study the Formula One advertisement and find in it as many of the techniques listed opposite as possible.

2 Try writing sentences against each of the techniques for either a theme park or Sydney, featured in Unit 4.

WORD WORK

Spellings: Science

First, test each other on the Art, Design and Technology spellings from Unit 6. Then, learn these tricky spellings to use in Science:

1 Physics

2 Apparatus

3 Liquefy

4 Alkaline

5 Acidic

6 Molecule

7 Pressure

8 Chemical

9 Oxygen

10 Breath/breathe

11 Resistance

13 Laboratory

14 Nutrient

15 Particle

16 Thermometer

17 Vertebrate

APPLE – APPARATUS. Link the two words to remember the double P.

Puzzle

Find within the words above:

3 rodents	2 mammals
3 school subjects	A naughty child
An American mother	French for nothing
French for green	The art of public speaking

Can you find others? Answers on page 135.

Know the difference: 'Affect' or 'effect'?

Special __ffects

Smoking adversely
__ffects your health

> Affect or effect? Affect is a verb.
> To affect something is to influence it.
>
> Effect is a noun. The effect is the result.

Don't let me __ffect your
decision

The __ffect of
microwaving an egg

Check your answers on page 135.

Words at work: Tautology

A tautology is the unnecessary use of words to repeat an idea. For
example:

> We collaborated together to produce a design.

Together is an unnecessary word because *collaborate* already means working together.

Activity

Find the tautologies in these sentences:

> *Researchers tracked back the idea to its original source.*
> *She returns back home.*
> *Delia reduces down the gravy by simmering it slowly in the pan.*
> *One day she will repay back the debt she owes.*
> *She is a very extraordinary woman.*
> *Settle up the bill.*
> *Repeat the same story to your father.*
> *The ship sank down to the sea bed.*
> *Follow after me.*
> *The neighbours have a past history of disagreements.*

- Study the words you could delete. Do you see any patterns?

- Study your own work for tautologies, and be aware of them over the next
  week or so.

DETECTIVE READER

Hearing the theme

The theme is what the book is about; its moral, message or the issue it dwells on. The theme runs all the way through a story, linking the events together. Books can have more than one theme.

Here are some common themes in books:

- growing up
- overcoming fear
- overcoming prejudice
- family harmony
- finding love
- foiling evil.

Can you think of any books you have read recently which have any of these themes?

Read the extract below and decide what might be the theme or themes of the story:

> By this example, the justice that was in the mind of Robin Hood began to dawn on his Merrie men. They began to understand that it was not Robin's intention to hurt ploughman or labourer. In fact, he had no wish to harm even a high-born knight who was honest and good. But if he knew of anyone cheating, or robbing, or lying, he aimed to mete out to the offender such justice as would be most fitting.
>
> "Help the good folk, and those who find life difficult," said Robin to his band; "but treat those who make it difficult as our enemies – with the Sheriff of Nottingham as the chief!"

From *Robin Hood and his Merrie Men*, Dean & Son Ltd

Check your answer on page 136.

Blurbs

The themes of a book are often mentioned in the back cover blurb. What do you learn from this blurb about the theme of the novel *Red Sky in the Morning*?

> Anna can't wait for her mother to give birth to the new baby – it's her big chance to show she's grown up and can take care of her dad and her younger sister. But the joy of the birth is touched with sadness when Ben is born handicapped.
>
> It's not easy when strangers stare. It's hard to explain at school. Yet Anna finds a deep love for Ben, a love that can show others that her little brother is beautiful, funny – and just the right person to teach her about life.

From *Red Sky in the Morning* by Elizabeth Laird

Endings

The theme of a book is often expressed in the ending. For example, a book about a girl being bullied at school might end in one of three ways:

A The girl learns to stand up for herself. One day, she helps the bully out, and they end up friends.

B The girl learns to stand up for herself and teaches the bully a lesson. The bully leaves for another school.

C The bullying gets worse. Everyone can see it, but no-one steps in because they are afraid. One day the girl is thrown against a kerb and dies of her injuries.

Which ending would suit which theme?

1 Complacency

2 Overcoming evil

3 Living in harmony

Activity

Here is another story line. Think of three endings to illustrate three different themes:

The boy Ivan escapes from a concentration camp and sets out on a journey of escape over the mountains to freedom. On his way, he must find food and shelter from people who have, so far, been his enemies.

WRITING SKILLS

Formality

Formal writing is polite but impersonal, and uses standard English. It is best used when:

- You do not know the person you are writing to

- When it is not a personal issue

- When the subject matter is official business.

Nonetheless, formal writing can be relaxed in tone and plain in style.

The exact tone and style will be determined by:

- The **purpose** for writing

- The **relationship with the reader**

- The **conventions** or writing style that is commonly expected in the situation.

Here are three items of mail received by Robert Kent on the same day.

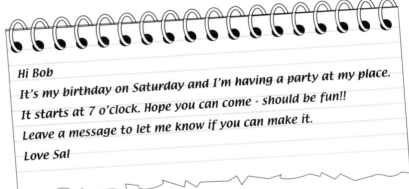

Hi Bob

It's my birthday on Saturday and I'm having a party at my place.

It starts at 7 o'clock. Hope you can come - should be fun!!

Leave a message to let me know if you can make it.

Love Sal

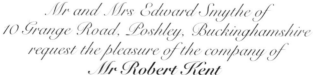

Wedding Invitation

Mr and Mrs Edward Smythe of
10 Grange Road, Poshley, Buckinghamshire
request the pleasure of the company of
Mr Robert Kent
at the wedding of their daughter
Sally Rose *to* **Mr Gregory Catchpole**
The Wedding Service is to take place at
11 am on Saturday 12th June
at
St. Thomas' Church, The Green, Quaintly
followed by a Champagne Reception at the Buckland Hotel, Poshley.
RSVP

The Club House,
Framley Park,
Framley,
Lancashire.
SK2 4EW

Robert Kent,
81, Lismore Road,
Dukinfield,
Cheshire.
SK16 4AZ

3rd March

Dear Mr Kent,

You may have heard that our colleague Sally Smythe is to be married in June this year. A number of us on the team have been invited and the committee feel it would be appropriate to buy a joint gift from the club members. If you wish to contribute, please send your cheque or postal order to Sid Baker at the above address. Sid has kindly offered to purchase a suitable gift. A card will be circulated at the May meeting.

I hope you are enjoying the current warm spell. I look forward to seeing you in May.

Yours sincerely,

Clare Parsons

Clare Parsons
Club secretary

What conventions can you see in these texts at:

- Text level – the lay out and organisation of the writing.

- Sentence level – the way it is expressed.

- Word level – spelling and vocabulary.

Standard English

The purpose of standard English is to be courteous and more formal by using a 'standard' form of English rather than a local or community dialect. There is nothing 'better' about standard English, but it is understood around the world, and in some situations, it is expected.

THE ART OF THE WRITER

Moving the plot along

Explanation:

In *planning*, you decide the main events and stages of the story, and establish the theme or moral of the story – what it is driving at.
In *writing*, you decide how to move the story along. There are five basic ways of doing this:

1 action

2 dialogue

3 description

4 narrative comment (when the narrator comments on events or speaks directly to the reader)

5 inner reflection (what the characters are thinking and feeling).

Though all writers have their favourite methods, most of them try to mix methods, choosing the one which can do the job best at that point.

Example

Here is an extract from a novel set during the war. Chas and his father are just coming out of an air raid shelter the morning after a bombing raid.

> At dawn, they climbed out stiffly. They were surprised to see their house still standing; and the rest of the houses in the Square. And the next row, beyond the long back-gardens, quite untouched except two were simply gone. The ones on either side were windowless, had slates missing. But two were simply gone.
>
> 'Ronnie Boyce lives there …' said Chas. He had given Ronnie Boyce a bloody nose two days ago.
>
> 'Did live there,' said his father. 'It was over quick. They can never have known what hit them.'
>
> Fat Ronnie Boyce, with his shiny boots and mum with asthma … where was he now? Up in heaven? With a harp and a halo to go with his shiny boots? He hoped God wasn't too rough on him. He was a terrible thief, but probably being blown to bits was enough punishment for being a thief.
>
> 'Chas, lad,' said his father, very quiet. 'I'm going to see if Nana and Granda are all right. Most of the stuff that was dropped fell by the river last night. I want you to come with me …'
>
> Chas felt his stomach go heavy, as if he'd swallowed a cannon-ball. Not Nana and Granda too! He saw in his mind their neat house in Henry Street, with the white wheel for a gate, and the big white seashells in the garden, and the freshly-painted flagstaff where his granda ran up the Union Jack every morning and saluted it.

From *The Machine Gunners* by Robert Westall

Activity

- Go through each sentence and decide which of the five methods it is using. Sometimes you may feel there is an overlap.

- Discuss why the writer chose inner reflection for the sentence: *Chas felt his stomach …*

- Discuss why the writer chose dialogue for the sentence: *'Did live there …'*

- Inner reflection is the most neglected method in school writing.

- Dialogue is useful when the plot is driven by the characters, especially if events are sparked off by something they say. Think hard before you use it. Is it the best way to move the plot along?

Dialogue

- Try reading the extract as a play script, just picking out the dialogue. What is lost?

- Now trying reading it without the dialogue. What is lost?

You should find that the dialogue is crucial to understanding. A good test of dialogue is that your work would not make sense without it. It is used to move the story along.

Dialogue is useful because:

- It is immediate, on the spot, as things happen.

- It shows the human side of events – and readers are naturally nosey!

- You learn more about characters if you can hear the way they express themselves.

For more about dialogue, look at Unit 10.

Try it

Write the next half page of the story, in which Chas and his father go round to Nana and Granda's house. Use at least four of the methods.

WRITING STYLE

A sentence to borrow: verbs

Here are four sentences from a fantasy adventure. There is something unusual about the order of words in the sentences. Can you see what they have in common?

> The eerie, unsettling hush deepened.

> Up into a glimmering space the nightmare creature lumbered.

> Consumed with hate and malice, the great inhuman arms lifted the rusted spear high over the ice-crested head, then down it plunged.

> With bursts of blinding fire, each of the glittering, fate-filled threads was severed and snapped.

Sentences from *The Fatal Strand* by Robin Jarvis

In each sentence, the last word is a verb. This has the effect of putting a great deal of emphasis on that verb, and of keeping the reader waiting to find out what actually happens. You can check this by trying to replace the last verb with a different word. For example:

The eerie, unsettling hush   … evaporated.

                                … was broken by voices.

                                … suddenly turned into loud music.

                                … continued.

Try replacing 'severed and snapped' to alter the meaning of the final sentence.

The technique of leaving the verb till last is borrowed from early oral story-tellers, who used it to keep their listeners on the edge of their seats. The earliest written stories, usually myths and legends, borrowed the trick. More recently, stories set in fantasy worlds of wizards and strange creatures have started to use it again. It gives an old world story-telling feel to the writing.

Valuable verbs

Good writers make their verbs work hard in a number of ways:

- Choosing powerful, precise verbs.

- Choosing verbs for their sound effect, e.g. onomatopaeia, alliteration.

- Positioning them in the sentence for best effect.

- Deciding whether it is an active (doing) verb or passive (done to) verb.

- Choosing tense.

- Adding adverbs.

Pick out the main verbs in this passage.

> Shrieking with blaspheming laughter, the Frost Giant surged forward, the spear raised above its malformed skull. Squealing, Edie Dorkins rushed in front of the Loom to protect it, but the unstoppable force of the ice lord knocked her aside and the girl was sent reeling.
>
> At once Gogus snapped and barked, pouncing on to one of the monster's legs and scampering up over the distorted back to claw and bite, thrashing the horror's face with its long tail. But the fiend was oblivious to that insignificant onslaught. Consumed with hate and malice, the great, inhuman arms lifted the rusted spear high over the ice-crested head, then down it plunged.

From *The Fatal Strand* by Robin Jarvis

Activity

Comment on each verb saying why it has been chosen and positioned where it is.

NON-FICTION

Bias

We are used to thinking of non-fiction as factual and therefore truthful. But even non-fiction can be presented in a biased way. A writer can influence your attitude by:

- selecting only some of the information

- concealing information

- playing up or making light of certain information

- presenting information as fact when it is only conjecture

- using words and phrases which influence the reader's attitude

- arranging facts so that they appear linked, prompting the reader to jump to conclusions.

It is not wrong to have a point of view, or to promote it. In writing non-fiction, you have a special responsibility to justify views and to distinguish between fact and opinion.

Example

Here is an article from a local newspaper. Local newspapers have a particularly tricky job because they need to represent the news accurately, but also wish to reflect the views and interests of the local population.

CASTLE GARDEN PICNICKERS MAY BE ASKED TO PAY

VISITORS to Rochester Castle gardens may have to pay up for the privilege.

Picnickers and tourists could now have to fork out for enjoying the peace and tranquillity of the gardens.

A report to the city council into Medway's tourist attractions suggested a fee as a means of raising revenue.

Other projects suggested by the report include building a roof over the castle, axing unpopular attractions and spending more than £100,000 to create tourist hubs in Rochester and the World Naval Base, Chatham.

And, in a further radical step, the report says money could be made by charging schools to visit Medway's historic sites.

Adscene week ending Friday 14 July 2000

Activity

Discuss:

- In what ways the article is reporting the facts of the case.

- In what ways it is expressing the likely views of the local population.

- Which aspects of language reflect the likely anxieties of local people about the proposal.

- Which aspects of language suggest a factual report.

Return to the list at the top of the page and find any examples in the article.

Primary sources

History is a subject in which we expect to find facts. A good historian looks to first-hand or primary sources for information. Because they were written at the time, they offer a close-up view of life and events when they happened. Yet even they are not completely reliable or truthful.

Here is an interesting example, because you, a modern reader, are likely to be sympathetic to Elizabeth Bentley, a woman who was interviewed about her work in a mill as part of the investigation into conditions in textile factories in 1832. The investigation led to changes in the law about working conditions in Victorian factories.

What age are you?
– **Twenty–three.**
Where do you live?
– **At Leeds.**
What time did you begin work at a factory?
– **When I was six years old.**
At whose factory did you work?
– **Mr. Busks.**
What kind of mill is it?
– **Flax–mill.**
What was your business in that mill?
– **I was a little doffer.**
What were your hours of labour in that mill?
– **From 5 in the morning till 9 at night.**
What time was allowed for your meals?
– **Forty minutes at noon.**
Had you any time to get your breakfast or drinking?
– **No, we got it as we could.**
Suppose you flagged a little, or were too late, what would they do?
– **Strap us.**
Girls as well as boys?
– **Yes.**
Have you ever been strapped?
– **Yes.**
Severely?
– **Yes.**

Activity

The instincts of a modern reader are to trust the interview and to recognise the cruelty of the factories. The interview is a primary source, and we have no reason to think she is lying. But what about the questioner?

- How and why have the questions been chosen? What is the questioner after?

- Could the questioner have asked a different set of questions that would have made us more sympathetic to the factory?

- How might a mill owner have answered similar questions about conditions in his mill?

- Someone wrote down the words spoken. Can you think of any way that this might influence the passage?

WORD WORK

Spellings: Music

First, test each other on the Science spellings from Unit 8.
Then, learn these tricky spelling to use in Music:

1 Choir
2 Choral
3 Chord
4 Crotchet
5 Lyrics
6 Minim
7 Minor
8 Musician
9 Orchestra
10 Synchronise

Puzzles

1 Find two words that could be extended to make new words unrelated to music.

2 Musical terms have more than their fair share of words containing 'CH'. Even more peculiar, they are usually sounded like 'K' rather than the more common soft sound (as in *chair*). Why is that?

3 Take three minutes in groups to see how many musical terms you can think of ending in a vowel. Hint: Think of musical instruments and words to describe how the music should be played. Get five bonus points if you can say why there are so many.

4 Music → musician. Find other professions which end in 'CIAN'.

Check your answers on page 136.

Know the difference: 'Much' or 'many'?

Use *how many* for items you can count separately, e.g. six apples. If someone asked 'How many?' you would reply with a number.

Use *how much* for general measurements, e.g. two kilos. If someone asked 'How much?' you would reply with an amount.

How much often refers to loose goods such as flour or sugar.

Compare:

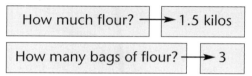

| How much flour? | → | 1.5 kilos |
| How many bags of flour? | → | 3 |

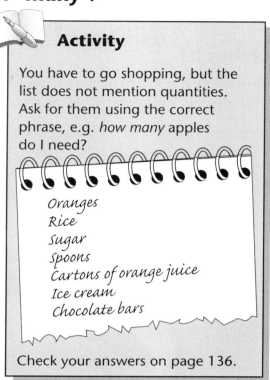

Activity

You have to go shopping, but the list does not mention quantities. Ask for them using the correct phrase, e.g. *how many* apples do I need?

Oranges
Rice
Sugar
Spoons
Cartons of orange juice
Ice cream
Chocolate bars

Check your answers on page 136.

Words at work: Sound effects

Word are composed of sounds and writers exploit this when they choose and use words. Match up the jumbled terms, definitions and examples:

TERMS	DEFINITIONS	EXAMPLES
rhyme	Where the emphasis falls in a word.	Hiss Crackle
onomatopoeia	Words which share the same consonant or vowel sounds.	/ - / - Pitter patter
assonance	Words which repeat the initial sound.	**In**jury In**her**it Reg**re**t
stress	Words which sound like the thing they describe.	The <u>s</u>oft <u>s</u>ighing of the the <u>s</u>ea
rhythm	Words which share an identical sound in the last syllable.	Killed, culled Moon, root
alliteration	The beat or pattern of stress.	Womb & tomb Great & hate

DETECTIVE READER

Living it!

We have seen in Unit 8 that good readers bring the text alive by thinking and feeling their way into it. The writer has created these sensations using only words. But how?

Shipwreck!

I fell on my hands and feet where the water was a yard deep under the ship, but got my footing and floundered through the water in a desperate struggle to climb as high as might be on the beach before the next wave came in. I saw the string of men lashed together and reaching down as far as man might, to save any that came through the surf, and heard them shout to cheer us, and watched a coil of rope flung out. Elzevir was by my side and saw it too, and we both kept our feet and plunged forward through the quivering slack water; but then there came an awful thunder behind, the crash of the sea over the wreck, and we knew that another mountain wave was on our heels. It came in with a swishing roar, a rush and rise of furious water that swept us like corks up the beach, till we were within touch of the rope's–end and the men shouted again to hearten us as they flung it out. Elzevir seized it with his left hand and reached out his right to me. Our fingers touched, and in that very moment the wave fell, with an awful suck, and I was swept down the beach again.

From Moonfleet by J. Meade Falkner

What's going on?

There's a lot of detail in the extract, and a sense of panic and confusion. But you still need to know what is going on. Go through it sentence by sentence, and pick out the basic events. Record this as a flow chart, using no more than two or three words for each entry. Your flow chart may look like this, for example:

Jumps in water a yard deep

↓

Struggles up beach

↓

How do we experience it?

> ### Activity
>
> 1 This is an extract told in the first person as 'I'. What can you work out about 'I'? E.g. Gender, age, background. What in the extract gives you these impressions?
>
> 2 The writer has made sure that we see the terrifying experience through the narrator's eyes. How does he create a sense of fear and threat? Find:
> - three phrases which emphasise the helplessness of their struggle in the water
> - seven phrases which emphasise the power and terror of the storm
> - four words which describe the sea with words we usually use for people.
>
> 3 Sometimes the survivors make headway, and the sentences tell us what they did. In this case, the sentences are structured so that they do the doing. The verbs are carried out by the two people in the water. For example: 'I fell on my hands and feet'.
> Sometimes the sea has the upper hand, and then the verbs refer to the sea. For example: 'It came in a swishing roar …' or 'There was an awful thunder behind …'. Go through the extract and decide when the balance of power shifts in the sentences.

Try to repeat this activity with the next extract in which the story continues:

> Yet the under-tow did not take me back to sea, for amid the floating wreckage floated the shattered maintop, and in the truck of the great spar I caught, and so was left with it upon the beach thirty paces from the men and Elzevir. Then he left his own assured salvation, namely the rope, and strode down again into the very jaws of death to catch me by the hand and set me on my feet. Sight and breath were failing me; I was numb with cold and half dead from the buffeting of the sea; yet his giant strength was powerful enough to save me then, as it had saved me before. So when we heard once more the warning crash and thunder of the returning wave we were but a fathom distant from the rope. "Take heart, lad," he cried; "'tis now or never," and as the water reached our breasts gave me a fierce shove forward with his hands. There was a roar of water in my ears, with a great shouting of the men upon the beach, and then I caught the rope.

WRITING SKILLS

See what you mean

If notes are made to assist memory, then recording notes in the form of drawing and diagrams can help because:

- You can see the shape or structure of the whole.

- Many people find it easier to read a diagram.

- It is quick.

It is well known that people learn better if they have both words and pictures to help them.

Diagrammatic notes are useful for:

- Visualising a scene or description, e.g. a stage set.

- Recording the stages of a process, e.g. manufacturing a product.

- Mapping the different aspects of a topic, e.g. different branches of science.

- Mapping relationships between one thing and another, e.g. a family tree.

Try it

Task 1

Here is an extract from the North West Water Company's web site:

> Only 1% of the Earth's water is freshwater, found in rivers and lakes, and it is this 1% that we all depend on for the water we need. This is the same as just 10 days rainfall, but thanks to the Water Cycle it doesn't get used up but goes round and round, naturally recycling.
>
> Energy from the sun reaches the water in the oceans, seas, rivers and lakes. Some water evaporates and becomes water vapour. As the vapour rises it gets colder and condenses into droplets of liquid. Billions of droplets group together to form clouds. The droplets merge until they are so heavy they fall back down as rain. Reservoirs collect the water as it runs off the hills and store it until it is needed.
>
> Although water is given to us by nature it always has to be purified before it is safe to drink. Taking away and treating wastewater is essential for both personal hygiene and public health. Clean wastewater is returned to rivers and the sea.

Identify nine stages in this water cycle, and note them on a circular diagram like the one opposite. Next to each stage draw a simple diagram to aid memory. One has been done for you.

1. *sun heats water*

Task 2

Here is an account of how Romans built roads. Take notes by drawing and labelling a cross section.

Roman roads were built to be strong, straight and hard-wearing. Two parallel trenches were dug and the earth piled between them. This meant that the road was high up, and people could see around as they walked along. On top of the earth, the Romans piled a layer of chalk if it was available because it helped to drain away the rain water. Next they piled a layer of flint because it was hard. Then they piled a rubble of small stones, and a top layer of small pebbles or gravel. This layer was rounded on the top with a camber to allow the rainwater to drain into the trenches.

Task 3

Here is an account of a farm. Draw a labelled map or plan to show the lay-out.

The farm buildings were dominated by the great house, where Mr Lennox and his daughters lived. It was approached by a long and wide drive which ended in a loop in front of the house so that coaches might turn. About a hundred years ago, the house was extended to form an L shape, and the new wing contained a dairy, stables and a store house. Mr Lennox's father had made further additions soon after his marriage, creating a new wing facing the old one, and although it was shorter than the other, it formed a courtyard of sorts. The new wing housed hay, winter crops and additional servants' quarters close to the house. Mrs Lennox had recently added a feature of her own: a fine arch 200 feet from the house, which she adored, but everyone else considered out of character with its surroundings and an obstruction of the view.

Activity

What kind of visual record would suit:

- a playwright's instructions for a stage set?

- an account of a production line?

- a history of the Hundred Years War?

- the life cycle of a bee?

- a design idea for a new house?

THE ART OF THE WRITER

Developing plot

There is a traditional shape for a story:

● Introduction which establishes characters, setting, and sets the events in motion.

● Problem develops.

● Problem intensifies and builds up.

● Conflict or crisis occurs.

● Change – the aftermath in which characters and events work through the new situation.

● Resolution – characters and events find a way to deal with the new situation.

The *exciting* bit is the conflict but the *interesting* bit is the problem which develops into a crisis and how people cope with it all afterwards. Every reader knows what it means to live with problems and tensions, and a good writer appeals to this natural human interest.

There are four ways to manage the interesting parts of the story better:

1 Make the reader empathise or identify with the problem.

2 Put the reader in suspense.

3 Make the reader work at the solution.

4 Make the reader wait for the solution.

Try it

Consider how you might do this in the following plots:

A woman visits a detective because her husband has disappeared without trace and without warning. Half way through the story, it will emerge that he has been spotted in a remote part of the world. What could the writer focus on between the woman telling her story and the first sighting?

A boy and girl fall in love despite the fact that their families hate each other. They marry in secret. Half way through the story, the boy kills his wife's cousin in a street fight and has to leave. The writer wants to keep the reader in suspense until the end but that will be hard because the lovers are separated! What could the writer focus on during the second half of the story?

Example

Here is an extract from a detective story about Sherlock Holmes.
The art of writing a detective story is to keep the reader guessing at
solutions, so they have well-developed stages of problem-building and
problem-solving:

"There is something which I don't understand in this matter. If ever a
man was three parts mad with terror, that man's name is Pinner.
What can have put the shivers on him?"

"He suspects that we are detectives," I suggested.

"That's it," said Pycroft.

Holmes shook his head. "He did not turn pale. He *was* pale when
we entered the room," said he. "Its is just possible that_____"

His words were interrupted by a sharp rat-tat from the direction of
the inner door.

"What the deuce is he knocking at his own door for?" cried the
clerk.

Again and much louder came the rat-tat-tat. We all gazed
expectantly at the closed door. Glancing at Holmes I saw his face
turn rigid, and he leaned forward in intense excitement. Then
suddenly came a low gurgling, gargling sound and a brisk drumming
upon the woodwork. Holmes sprang frantically across the room and
pushed at the door. It was fastened on the inner side. Following his
example, we threw ourselves upon it with all our weight. One hinge
snapped, then the other, and down came the door with a crash.
Rushing over it, we found ourselves in the inner room.

It was empty.

But it was only for a moment that we were at fault.

From *The Adventure of the Stockbroker's Clerk* by Sir Arthur Conan Doyle

Activity

- Look back to the four points which list the ways of
  managing problem-building and problem-solving and
  identify where and how these are used in this extract.

- Continue the story for two more paragraphs but don't
  'solve' the problem. Practise building up the reader's
  anticipation and search for a solution.

WRITING STYLE

A technique to borrow: similes

In these sentences, the writer has used simile to add instant associations to their descriptions. Similes are risky because many of them are over-used, but they are a quick way of describing what something is like without spending many words on it.

> Like a great galumphing goose, she spun around and stomped through the room, flapping her arms and shaking her head so that her long plaits whisked madly about her face.

> Many of them were wraithlike in appearance, wavering between starvation and death.

> Sucking the air between his teeth, his eyes still firmly closed, the old man lifted his head to the ceiling and became as still as stone.

Sentences from *The Fatal Strand* by Robin Jarvis

Activity

- Identify the similes.

- Identify in each sentence at least one other way in which the writer extends the simile by alluding to it again.

Try writing these sentences using a simile and then extending it in at least one other word or phrase in the sentence:

1 A sentence describing a teacher in terms of a predatory animal.
2 A sentence describing a person in terms of a small mammal.
3 A sentence describing a road in terms of a snake.
4 A sentence describing a thinking person in terms of a computer.

Study this extract and identify at least six examples of one thing being described in terms of another:

> In the corner of his eye, the boy saw the man's lumbering bulk gaining on him and, as he sprang across the gap between one loom and its neighbour, he felt the frame judder and tilt as the weapon thumped in behind. Only one more short dash and he would reach the door. Once through, he would flee from this hellish place and the overseer would never catch him.
>
> Scrabbling under the final obstacle, Ned suddenly heard a violent tearing as the silk was ripped from the warp above. Before he could hare away, Obediah's brawny arms flashed inside and a huge hand gripped one of the boy's spindly legs.
>
> "Got you!" the man spat, hauling the lad up through the shredded fabric in one ferocious movement. "You'll be sorry you went a-thievin' today – but not for long."
>
> Hanging upside down in the braggart's iron grasp, Ned kicked out with his free leg and swung his fists, but the evil man only let out a course, braying laugh at his puny struggles.
>
> "A catcher of vermin," he guffawed. "That's what I am! One more rat a-goin' to get its brains bashed in."

From *The Fatal Strand* by Robin Jarvis

Try writing a paragraph or two of your own describing a chase, in which the pursuer is described in terms of an animal predator and the pursued in terms of prey.

NON-FICTION

Planning an essay

Success in tests relies on your ability to show what you know. You can't win marks if you can't explain yourself clearly and logically. The essay is simply a piece of extended writing in which you show what you know. Here is a sequence for planning an essay:

1 Pay attention to the question – what is it asking for?

2 Brainstorm – bring to mind everything you know about the subject.

3 Identify the main points you will make in the essay.

4 Decide on a structure for the essay – how you will organise and link the points.

5 Collect and cluster ideas, examples, evidence and details around the main points.

6 Rehearse the opening lines for each paragraph.

7 Fill in any gaps or imbalances in the plan.

Hot Tips

1 Find the key word in the question

It's easy to spot the topic, but what sort of approach is it asking for? Spot the key word such as:

| EXPLAIN | DESCRIBE | DISCUSS | OUTLINE | JUSTIFY |

- Can you think of others?

- Identify the key words in the following essay titles:

A Explain how the abolition of child labour was brought about in Britain.

B Discuss why it took so long to abolish child labour in Britain.

C Argue the case for the abolition of child labour in Victorian Britain.

D Justify the view that child labour is morally wrong.

- What differences would you face deciding and organising the main points of these essays?

- How would the topic influence the tone and style of your writing?

2 Prompt yourself

Try giving yourself a prompt, e.g. Child labour is wrong because ..., then try to complete the sentence in as many ways as possible. Try it with these prompts:

Child labour is wrong because ...

Farming is a rewarding career because ...

It took ages to abolish child labour because ...

3 Plan around a diagram

Jot notes to remind yourself of things to mention.

- Flow charts – good for sequences, cause and effect, order of events, instructions.
- Grids – good when there are more than two things to consider or compare.
- Columns – good for comparing or contrasting two things.
- Star charts – good for topics, factual information, subjects with many angles to consider.
- Timeline – good for history, chronological events, topics in which timing is important.

Decide what kind of diagram you would use to plan these essays:

A Compare the fighting methods of the Greeks and the Romans.

B Describe the decline of the Roman empire.

C Explain how the mail service processes letters from from post-box to letter-box.

D Write a leaflet to help a child choose an appropriate pet.

E What makes Spain the most popular holiday destination for British holiday-makers?

4 Brainstorm handy phrases

It's worth spending half a minute jotting down phrases you might use. This will stop you automatically using the same phrase again and again. For example, for an essay presenting a point of view:

There is a clear case for …	One reason is …
Most reasonable people would accept that …	Evidence suggests …
This view is confirmed by …	Some may say… but …
Consequently …	Similarly …
This tells us …	Furthermore …
Therefore …	

What phrases might be handy to:

- reject a point of view?
- express some reservations without actually disagreeing?

5 Check

Check your main points. For each one, ask:
    What do you mean?
    Prove it!
    Is that all?
    So what's your point?

WORD WORK

Spellings: Common errors

First test yourself of the Music spellings from Unit 9.

Then, test yourself on these tricky but common spellings, and find a way to learn the ones you don't know.

1	Alcohol	9	Exercise	17	Conscience
2	Aerial	10	Guard	18	Conscious
3	Vaccination	11	Guitar	19	Sincerely
4	Beginning	12	Necessary	20	Answer
5	Tomorrow	13	Definitely	21	Accident
6	Cemetery	14	Separate	22	Distinguish
7	Medicine	15	February	23	Fascism
8	Luggage	16	Library		

Know the difference: 'EX' or 'EXC'?

Most words start with 'EX' rather than 'EXC'. 'EX' is Latin for outside or leave, hence:

- Exit
- Exhale
- Expel
- Export

Can you think of other 'EX' words which have the meaning *leave* or *outside*?

A number of words start with 'EXC'. Often you can hear the 'C' so it is easy to spell. For example:

Excavate

Exclude

Sometimes the 'C' is soft and hard to hear. You need to learn these words:

Except

Excellent

Exceed/excess

Excite

A rhyme to help you remember:

I'm exceedingly excited
To be playing for United
And except for saving penalties,
I'm excellent in goal.

Words at work: Key words in essay titles

As you have seen, essay titles often use a key word which tells you how to organise an essay. Match the words to the definitions then check your answers on page 136:

A Discuss

B Explain

C Demonstrate

D Compare

E Contrast

F Evaluate

G Trace

H Argue

I Describe

J Explore

K Justify

1 Prove with evidence.

2 Prove the case for.

3 List the key elements and help the reader to see the links between them.

4 Make a considered judgement and explain it in detail.

5 Show by example exactly how something works.

6 Define the differences.

7 Clarify the main issues by going through them, saying what is significant and interesting about them, weighing them against one another and taking account of different views.

8 Go through the issues, saying what is significant and interesting about them, making connections and coming to tentative conclusions.

9 Define the similarities.

10 Give a full picture.

11 Follow something from its origins and through its stages of development.

Activity

Discuss how you might organise your answer to these questions:
- Trace the development of Joe's character in the novel.
- Discuss the issues raised by the use of the internet by under-12s.
- Argue the case for banning the use of the internet by under-12s.
- Explain the ending of the film "2001: A Space Odyssey".
- Evaluate the ending of the film "2001: A Space Odyssey".

DETECTIVE READER

Active reader

Good readers are active readers. They don't just sponge up the text, they help to make it happen! To show how this works, read the following extract, in which a young boy is surprised by a man whilst he is playing in a marshy place. Notice all the things your brain does as you read. For example, you may find that you:

● Hear a voice reading in your head.

● Remember people, places and events from your own life.

What else do you do? Try reading it twice, and watch what is going on in your head.

> "Hold your noise!" cried a terrible voice, as a man started up from among the graves at the side of the church porch. "Keep still, you little devil, or I'll cut your throat!"
>
> A fearful man, all in coarse grey, with a great iron on his leg. A man with no hat, and with broken shoes, and with an old rag tied round his head. A man who had been soaked in water, and smothered in mud, and lamed by stones, and cut by flints, and stung by nettles, and torn by briars; who limped, and shivered, and glared and growled; and whose teeth chattered in his head as he seized me by the chin.
>
> "O! Don't cut my throat, sir," I pleaded in terror. "Pray don't do it, sir."
>
> "Tell us your name!" said the man. "Quick!"
>
> "Pip, sir."

From *Great Expectations* by Charles Dickens

What was going on in your head? You may find that you:

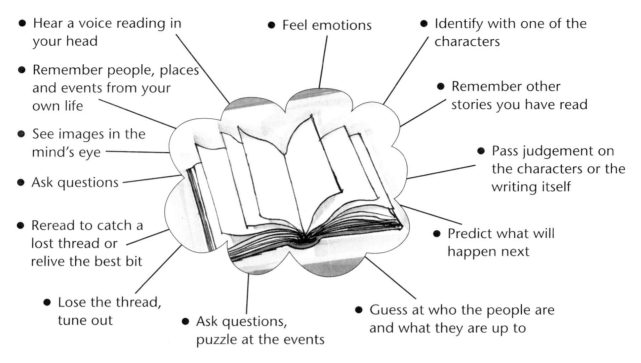

- Hear a voice reading in your head
- Remember people, places and events from your own life
- See images in the mind's eye
- Ask questions
- Reread to catch a lost thread or relive the best bit
- Lose the thread, tune out
- Ask questions, puzzle at the events
- Feel emotions
- Identify with one of the characters
- Remember other stories you have read
- Pass judgement on the characters or the writing itself
- Predict what will happen next
- Guess at who the people are and what they are up to

Compare your reading with two or three other people:

- Compare the images you saw in your mind's eye. They will be similar in many ways because the author told you some things to 'see'. But how do you account for the differences?

- Who did you identify with? Again your answers will be similar because the author rigged it to be that way. How?

Try this activity again with this extract in which The Hobbit, Bilbo, is on his way to face a fearsome dragon called Smaug.

It was at this point that Bilbo stopped. Going on from there was the bravest thing he ever did. The tremendous things that happened afterwards were as nothing compared to it. He fought the real battle in the tunnel alone, before he ever saw the vast danger that lay in wait. At any rate, after a short halt, go on he did; and you can picture him coming to the end of the tunnel, an opening of much the same size and shape as the door above. Through it peeps the hobbit's little head. Before him lies the great bottom-most cellar or dungeon-hall of the ancient dwarves right at the mountain's root. It is almost dark so that its vastness can only be dimly guessed, but rising from the near side of the rocky floor there is a great glow. The glow of Smaug.

From *The Hobbit* by J. R. R. Tolkien

WRITING SKILLS

Checking

Everyone knows that you need to check work for errors, but the method of checking should be suited to you.

Consider the different types of error that occur when you write:

- Forgetting to say something important.

- Realising you said the wrong thing.

- Spelling and punctuation errors.

- Slips and accidents.

- Personal bugbears – things you know you always get wrong.

Tips for successful checking

1 Read it aloud in your head

- Read back your own writing to hear a speaking voice inside your head. Listen for false notes and weak expression.

- Imagine your teacher sitting listening to you – the reactions of this imaginary being will help you to know if you've got the tone right.

2 Learn a list of your own most common errors

For example, if you know that your common weakness is to:

- wander from the margin when starting new lines

- mix up 'there' and 'their'

- forget to justify your opinions,

- forget to leave paragraph breaks

then use a mnemonic or memory trick to remember these four things and write them on the top of your sheet where you can rub them out later. This will remind you to be alert for your most likely errors.

Wander over *there* … you're *justified* in taking a *break*.

3 Space to put things right

If you find it hard to start, and this is often the worst part of your writing, try leaving a gap at the beginning of an essay or answer, and move on to the answer itself. Later, go back and write an introduction that sums up and leads into the points you know you are going to make.

If you know that you forget points, leave lines between each paragraph so there is somewhere you can add in last minute points.

Leave a gap between answers in an examination so that you can add things in when you come to check.

4 Spell scan

If spelling is your problem, know your most common types of error and search them out, e.g. longer words and plurals.

Scan rather than read, looking for that type of word.

5 Skimming for slips

To pick up slips, you need to skim through quickly but in full, concentrating on the parts that you wrote quickly and the parts that were the most tricky to write. Slips happen at these times because your mind is concentrating on something else.

THE ART OF THE WRITER

Dialogue

Dialogue is one of five story-telling methods studied in Unit 8. Dialogue is useful because:

- It can move the plot along if it is used instead of action.

- There is human interest in 'eavesdropping' on conversation.

- Characters are developed through the way they speak and what they say.

- You find out about relationships from the way people speak to each other.

Dialogue is not simply speech. The speech is often embedded in a longer sentence which may, for example, tell the reader *who* is speaking and *how* they speak.

Here is an extract of dialogue from a novel set in the war. Stan has brought Police Officer Green to see something strange about the wreck of a German aircraft:

Why I brought you here, sir ... look at this.' He pointed to an aluminium spar still sticking out of the wreckage.

'Sawn through with a hacksaw,' said Stan. 'Now what would have been attached to that, sir?'

'Machine-gun, I suppose.'

'And there's ammunition missing, too. These planes carry 2000 spare rounds in the rear gun-position. I checked with RAF Acklington.'

'But who could have pinched them?'

'Look at that hacksaw-cut. Can you imagine a grown-up being that cack-handed? I reckon it's kids, sir.'

'Oh, surely...'

'What about that then, sir?' Green pointed to the bullet-holes in the rudder handing overhead.

'Made by the fighter that shot him down.'

'Wrong calibre. They're 7.62 millimetre. The RAF use .303'

'Then the gunner shot through his own tail in a panic!'

'The angle's impossible. Those holes were made when the machine-gun was already detached from the plane. One of my beat bobbies actually heard it happen, the night after the plane was shot down.'

> 'Why didn't he investigate?'
>
> 'He didn't know what it was, and then the siren went. He thought it was part of the raid. I'm afraid he's not very bright.'
>
> 'You mean…'
>
> 'Some bright kid's got a gun and 2000 rounds of live ammo.'

From *The Machine Gunners* by Robert Westall

Activity

- There are only three embedded narrative comments in this extract. Find them and explain why the writer was forced to drop out of dialogue to use narrative instead of dialogue.

- Bearing in mind that there is so little help from the narrator, how do you keep track of who is talking? Make a list of ways you can help the reader.

- Find the places where the characters are mentioned by name or title either by the narrator or by each other, and what they reveal about the relationship between the two characters.

- What else do you learn about the two men from their conversation?

Try writing a few lines of dialogue for each of these situations:

- An awkward conversation between two embarrassed people trapped together in a lift, waiting for help to arrive.

- A man surprised at his door by a television crew for a game show. His mates have secretly entered him in a competition.

- A daughter telling her parents that she has decided to leave home.

WRITING STYLE

A sentence to borrow: clustering

Sentences can be used to cluster up ideas, objects or actions to give a packed, busy feel to a scene.

Here is a sentence which clusters up the objects carried on Ben's back by listing them:

> Ben carried a canvas mountain tent, white felt boots, camouflage gear, pile jacket, and double sleeping bag.

In this sentence, Ben's routine tasks on the farm are listed, but it is not a list of objects but of actions:

> Ben made apple boxes out of pine shook, pulled weeds in the kitchen garden, split cordwood for the fireplace, and milked cows twice a day.

Here is another example which describes how Ben, a vet, examines an injured dog:

> Under the headlamp, working through the fur, following evidence of blood matted there, he took account of Rex's wounds: the left hamstring, between the hip and stifle, was punctured and swollen from hemorrhage; from shoulder to shoulder, low across the withers, a long run of skin had been ripped open, a gaping tear he could retract with his fingers to reveal the transparent fascia, the blunt tips of the spinal column, and the neat bone of the shoulder blades; and finally a broad tearing of the skin at Rex's throat, exposing one jugular.

What is listed and why are they clustered together in one sentence?

Consider also how and why the same writer has clustered together ideas in this extract:

> Renee would piece together his final hours, the way in which he'd lived them. She would hear about his swollen eye and ask questions of Ilse Peterson, who would relate the story of the wolfhounds and of the death of Tristan and the recovery of Rex, and certainly it would all seem strange.

The writer can signal 'clustering' links between sentences by:

- Repeating sentence structures

- Starting sentences in the same way

- Repeating words and sounds.

In the next extract, Ben is trying to diagnose the illness of a fellow-traveller who has fallen ill.

Identify 'clusters' in this extract and say how and why they are bound together:

There has been no rashes, no stiff, sore neck, no swollen throat. He had no lumps in his neck or armpits. He didn't smoke cigarettes and never had. He did not eat much, but in the last few days he'd had refried beans, a ham sandwich with salsa and onion, a stew of chicken backs, tortillas. He'd had coffee with sugar and milk that morning, some Kool-Aid and a Pepsi Cola. As much water as he could drink. Yes, they drank irrigation water at first. No, they didn't often wash their hands. Yes, they had all felt ill at times, mildly ill, from travelling. But the sick one had really begun to suffer about three weeks ago. He began to ache in his muscles and joints and was light-headed in the fields. He felt sleepy most of the time. Now he couldn't keep from coughing, especially in the night hours. They didn't know what to do with him.

All extracts in this section are taken from *East of the Mountains* by David Guterson

NON-FICTION

Making comparisons

When you are asked to compare two texts, it is important to know what aspects are for comparison. If none are defined, then you have to work out for yourself what the main points are. Generally in English, the topic of the passages will be the same, but the attitudes and the language will be different.

Compare these two newspaper reports. There are a hundred years between them. What differences can you see in the way disasters have been reported?

TERRIBLE EXPLOSION AT A HAT WORKS

The explosion took place in the "proofing" department, among the spirits used in the manufacture of hats. A larger number of workpeople were engaged in the premises, and the bodies of those killed were found scattered in different directions, presenting a ghastly spectacle. The rescuers came across six dead bodies, all mutilated beyond recognition.

Hundreds of people were engaged in the work of search with pickaxes and shovels. As they were recovered the remains of the dead workmen were removed to an outhouse. The injured were got out of the ruins with all possible despatch and transferred to the Manchester and Stockport infirmaries. With the exception of two, the whole of the killed were unmarried, the majority of them being youths whose ages ranged from fifteen to eighteen. Joseph Brooks, who was thirty-nine years of age, and James Shopley, who, apparently, was a little older, were the only victims who were married.

The disaster is stated to have occurred through some young men smoking in the works, contrary to express orders.

RAIDERS RAM SHOP FOR CASH MACHINE

A GROUP of ram raiders demolished a cash machine and made off with a safe in a daring attack.

Neighbours living opposite Grimps Newsagents in Wells Road, Strood, raised the alarm when a group of youths rammed the shop with a four wheel drive vehicle at 3am yesterday.

Newsagent Janice Cox was called by police in the early hours of the morning.

Mrs Cox from Cliffe Woods said: "We've only had the cash machine for two weeks.

"Everyone thought it was wonderful because we didn't have to go into Strood to get cash. It's not so wonderful now."

She added, "We can't understand how they did it – the shop is 3ft below the pavement and it's difficult to drive up to."

Mrs Cox and her husband Colin took over the newsagents three and a half years ago and have been the victims of two other break-ins.

Michael Kinnard who lives opposite was woken by the noise of the raiders.

He said: "I saw five teenagers outside the shop and called the police. As I was on the phone I saw the shop window pop out – I think they tied something to the cash machine."

An engineer who came to collect the broken Link machine said he could not understand how it had been so thoroughly demolished.

A spokesman from Securicor, the company which loaded the machine with cash, refused to reveal how much was taken.

Det Insp Dave Withers said: "The men caused a significant amount of damage to the shop."

	EXPLOSION	RAM RAIDERS
Text level • Structure/organisation • Sequence of points • Lay-out		
Sentence level • Viewpoint (first person 'I', third person, etc.) • Tense • Active 'I do'/passive 'It was done' • Typical sentence structure & length • Typical links, e.g. on the other hand		
Word level • Typical words or phrases • Specialised vocabulary • Elaborate or plain vocabulary		

Structure your analysis in the following order:

1 What the two texts are, and what they are about

2 Text level – similarities

3 Text level – differences

4 Sentence level – similarities

5 Sentence level – differences

6 Word level – similarities

7 Word level – differences

8 How the two texts reflect changes that have occurred over time.

ANSWERS

UNIT ONE
Word Work

1 Dial, mat, log, act, eat. You can also find: Thor (a Viking god), die, play, lay, right, rig, the, he, heat, at, no, to, top, try.

2 Prophecy (noun) prophesy (verb).

Device (noun) devise (verb).

Advice (noun) advise (verb).

Detective Reader

1 The main point is that it isn't unusual for film-goers to imagine that they are the film stars they have just been watching. The paragraph provides evidence in the form of examples.

2 The other main point is that Catherine knew it was her fault.

UNIT TWO
Word Work

1 Govern, over, men, Liam, am, or, for, fore, arch, ron, logic, log, cur, rent, depend, pen, dependence, end, den, lit, it, tar.

2 Sovereign, feign, deign.

3 Americans:

- Don't double the 'L' at the end of a word when they add to it, e.g. travel + er.

- Put 'ER' rather than 'RE' at the end of a word, e.g. centimeter.

- Drop French-style endings, e.g. program rather than programme.

Detective Reader

The uncle is probably an excellent motorbike mechanic who takes a real pride in his work. He keeps his garage tidy and cleans his tools lovingly after using them. The photographs on the wall remind him of bikes he's built in the past.

Writing Skills

Grendel:

1 One man was snoring – change of place and viewpoint.

2 For a moment – change of place and viewpoint.

3 Through half-closed eyes – change of viewpoint.

4 Grendel saw – change of viewpoint.

5 Still the Geats – change in topic and mood.

> This extract is very cinematic. The paragraphs act just as camera cuts would in a film, showing the action from a different perspective.

Musicals:

1 Musicals tell – opening.

2 There are many – change of topic from defining musicals to styles of musical.

3 Musicals began – change of topic and time.

4 The first film – change of topic and time.

5 Fashions changed – change of topic and time.

6 In the 1970s – change of topic and time.

> There isn't a new paragraph at 'The actual musical …' because the writer has not closed the topic. You will see that it is picked up again in the next sentence but one. The absence of the break warns you of this.

UNIT THREE
Word Work

Homophones – Hungary, Wales, Chile, Ireland

Homonym – Turkey, China, Chad

Writing Skills

Breathing

Breathing helps us to absorb life-giving oxygen into our blood. It also helps to remove carbon dioxide from our blood. Our breathing speeds up when we exercise and slows down when we are resting.

Inhaling

When we breathe we inhale, sucking air into our lungs. Oxygen in the air goes from the airspaces in our lungs and is absorbed into our blood.

Exhaling

We blow air out of our lungs when we exhale. Waste carbon dioxide is taken from our blood into the air spaces in our lungs. We get rid of this waste by breathing out.

A **key sentence** usually indicates the content of the rest of the paragraph, or gives the main point first. It leads the reader off in the right direction.

UNIT FOUR
Word Work

Temper

Neigh

Culture

Villa

Stationary – standing still

Stationery – paper, etc

Principal – main thing or person

Principle – moral or guideline

Passed – went by

Past – history

Currant – small fruit

Current – of the moment, or a flow

Writing Skills

Tom sold local and imported fruit.

UNIT FIVE
Word Work

Circ (round) – circle, circus, circumstance, circular

Dec (10) – decathlon, December (used to be tenth month), decimate (Roman practice of killing every 10th soldier as a punishment)

Para (like) – paramedic, paratrooper

Radi (around) – radiate, radius, radiation, radiator, radial

Meter (measure) – metric, centimetre, themometer

Quantifying

Very, intensely, rather, somewhat, slightly, a little, quite, extremely, greatly, likewise, similarly, considerably, generally,

Writing Skills

Suggestions (there are alternatives)

1 Angel liked Buffy, but decided to leave for a starring role in a new series.

2 Life was lonely for the commander's children. They were not allowed to play outside the camp. They took lessons from private tutors. Children learnt Latin and Greek. Lessons were hard. (*30 words*)

3 The joined version:
Life was lonely for the commander's children. They were not allowed to play outside the camp, and had hard lessons such as Latin and Greek from private tutors. (*28 words*)

UNIT SIX
Word Work

Prey/pray
Cymbal/symbol
Him/hymn
Profit/prophet

Triple homophones:

Detective Reader

Gwyn's grandmother is clearly upset with her grandson. She doesn't smile or look at him as you would expect but looks away, probably to hide her feelings or make him feel uncomfortable. Her tone is unfriendly. The writer describes her as speaking "coldly", and she sarcastically accuses him of neglecting her: "Don't let me detain you from your urgent business." She treats him like an intruder "snooping" and "lurking like a thief". She is deliberately trying to make Gwyn feel bad and in the end she gets what she wants because he feels guilty and wants to speak to her.

Non-fiction

Text	2 examples	Text level	Sentence level	Word level
Recount	D J	E	B	B
Instruction	A I	B	A	C
Information	E K	F	D	E
Explanation	H L	A	C	F
Persuasion	B F	C	F	A
Discursive writing	C G	D	E	D

UNIT SEVEN
Word Work

Design

Research

Texture

Technology

Alternative

Perspective

Vertical

Horizontal

Diagonal

Dimension

Engine

Machine

The ladies' coats – lots of ladies, lots of coats.
The dog's lead – one dog, and the lead belongs to it.
The teacher's pet – one teacher, one pet.
The teachers' books – lots of teachers, lots of books.

It's = it is

Its = belongs to it

There is no such word as *its'* because *it* is always singular. The plural of *it* is *they* or *them*. You would say *theirs* instead.

Art of the Writer

Clues:

- The iron on his leg is a shackle. He has broken the chain to escape, but still has the ring around his ankle.

- He is desperately hungry.

- He is ill-clothed in his grey prison uniform.

- He is scarred and battered with his escape run.

- He is lurking in a lonely graveyard to avoid detection.

Dickens leaves us to work this out because we are seeing the story through the eyes of a child. The narrator is too young to work it out for himself.

UNIT EIGHT
Word Work

3 rodents:	rat × 3
2 mammals:	Ox and mole
3 school subjects:	RE, Art, Physics
A naughty child:	brat
An American mother:	mom
French for nothing:	rien
French for green:	vert
The art of public speaking:	oratory

'Effect'/'Affect'

Special *effects*
Smoking adversely *affects* your health
Don't let me *affect* your decision
The *effect* of microwaving an egg

Detective Reader

The themes of Robin Hood are equality and social justice.

UNIT NINE
Word Work

1 Minimum, minority.

2 Many musical terms are taken from the Greek, in which 'CH' is pronounced in that way.

3 Duo, trio, piccolo, oboe, viola, andante, mezze, etc. Many musical terms are borrowed from Italian, in which vowel endings are very common.

4 Beautician, physician, mortician, politician, optician, mathematician.

Shopping list

How many oranges?

How much rice?

How much sugar?

How many spoons?

How many cartons of orange juice?

How much ice cream?

How many chocolate bars?

UNIT TEN
Word Work

A7, B3, C5, D9, E6, F4, G11, H2, I10, J8, K1.